JN102667

VOA News:

Readings for Cross-cultural Understanding
異文化理解のための VOA ニュース 15

瀧 由紀子／中島 和郎

Jay Ercanbrack ／ Jonathan Jackson

榎本 暁／齊藤 隆春／山内 優佳

EIHŌSHA

音声ファイルのダウンロード方法

英宝社ホームページ（http://www.eihosha.co.jp/）の
「テキスト音声ダウンロード」バナーをクリックすると、
音声ファイルダウンロードページにアクセスできます。

はじめに

　本書は、Voice of America (VOA) の Learning English と Student Union のニュースから異文化理解に関する最近のトピックを選び、リーディング教材として作成したものです。なおニュースの原文は、教育的な目的のために、多少修正しています。

　「英語を通して世界の人とわかりあう心」を持ち、「異文化を理解しようとする態度」を深めるために、学習者が世界各国で起こった社会・文化面の興味深い出来事を知り、自分の問題として考え、読み進めていけるように教材が編成されています。
　Chapter は全部で 15 あり、一つの Chapter には、平易な語彙と基本的な文法で構成された本文があり、そのあとの Notes で注意の必要な語彙の説明をしています。基礎固めが終わり、これから次のステップに進む学習者にとっても楽しみながら読み進められるレベルです。
　本書は 4 技能 (読む、聞く、話す、書く) 活動を通して、リーディングが学習できるようにバランスよく構成されています。特に、自分の意見を書いたり、話し合ったりする問題を作り、各トピックについて自分の中でさらに深め、英語を使って自己表現する機会を設けています。

特色として :

1. How many words do you know? では、本文を理解するのに必要な重要語の意味を選択肢から選び、内容理解に備えます。
2. Reading comprehension: True or False では、内容についての質問に答え、読解確認をします。
3. Grammar section では、各チャプターに出てくる重要な文法を丁寧に説明し、構文理解の手助けをしています。
4. Listen to the dialogue and fill in the blanks. では、本文の問題をさらに発展させた会話や、テーマに関連した会話を聞き、単語の聞き取りや pair work での会話練習をします。
5. What's your opinion? では、自分の意見を英語でまとめ pair work で話し合います。
6. Cultural Information: Do you know? では、トピックに関する補足情報を日本語で提供しています。

それでは、世界の国々のニュースの旅に出発してください。

最後に、本書の出版にあたり、適切な助言をいただいた英宝社編集部の下村幸一氏に心からお礼を申し上げます。

2020 年　9 月
著者一同

◆　CONTENTS　◆

Think Love is Complicated? Try Speaking Different Languages

恋人同士のコミュニケーションは母語でも難しいものです。異なる文化で育ち、異なる言語を話す恋人たちの間には、どのような難しさがあるのでしょうか。
※写真はイメージです。

The language of love is difficult and complicated, no matter where you're from. With more than one million international students enrolled in colleges and universities across the United States, sparks are bound to fly.

A pair of students, one of whom is an international student, was interviewed and asked to describe how they manage their romantic relationship.

Khea Chang's family emigrated from Taiwan to Vancouver, Canada, making her a first-generation Canadian studying international relations at Boston University. Justin Devuono is from an Italian American family and is studying computer science at Harvard University in Cambridge, Massachusetts.

When they met at a friend's party, Justin's first impression was that Khea was cute. They slowly got to know each other but were just friends at first. However, Justin describes himself as "a guy who always keeps his eyes open for new opportunities," so when he realized he had a chance to start a romantic relationship with Khea, he went for it.

Yet despite the fact that they were both born and raised in a Western culture, the differences between their families were significant and hard to conquer. "It takes a lot of communication and understanding," Khea said, recalling her first visit to Justin's family.

"Being from an Asian family, when you bring your significant other to meet them, they're always very reserved," Khea said. "But when I met Justin's family, they immediately took me in and warmed to me very quickly. This was something I was not used to and, frankly, that I was shocked by. The very first time they met me, they didn't hesitate to invite me to stay with them for Christmas."

For his part, Justin said he felt the most difficult part of maintaining their relationship was to communicate and form a meaningful relationship with Khea's family because they don't speak English. "The language barrier between me and her parents makes it hard to develop a personal connection," Justin said.

Cultural differences matter a lot in their relationship. Different family backgrounds make their communication harder because the values they hold and the ways they think differ significantly. Khea said that she had a hard time explaining her Chinese culture and roots to Justin.

"It's easy to get into fights with him simply because we have very different ways of doing things," she said. "For example, it was hard for him to understand the symbolism behind many Chinese customs. And for me, although my family is from Taiwan, I grew up in Canada, so even I can't thoroughly understand or explain some parts of the symbolism. I just use it because my family uses it." (437 words)

📝 NOTE

enroll: 入学する　sparks are bound to fly: きっと衝突が起こる　emigrate: 移住する　reserved: 控えめな　significant other: 恋人、大切な人　language barrier: 言葉の壁　symbolism: 象徴的な意味　thoroughly: 十分に

---

1 How many words do you know?

次の単語の意味を、右の選択肢から選び記号で答えなさい。

1. complicated	(　)	a. 機会
2. impression	(　)	b. ～をちゅうちょする
3. despite	(　)	c. 複雑な
4. opportunity	(　)	d. 印象
5. hesitate	(　)	e. 重大な・大きな影響を与える
6. maintain	(　)	f. ～を維持する
7. significant	(　)	g. ～にもかかわらず

2 Reading Comprehension: True or False

次の英文が、本文の内容に合っていればTを、合っていなければFを（　　）内に書きなさい。

1. Khea and Justin got to know each other when they attended the same class.

（　　　）

2. Justin wanted to start a relationship with Khea after they made friends with each other. （　　　）

3. When Khea first visited Justin's family, they were very reserved. （　　　）

4. Justin finds it hard to communicate with Khea's family because of language differences. （　　　）

5. Khea cannot explain some aspects of her family's cultural background to Justin because she does not fully understand them. （　　　）

3 Grammar section

「分詞構文の表す意味」

Being from an Asian family, you might expect your family to be reserved when you bring your significant other to meet them.

「アジア系の家の出身であれば、あなたが大事な相手を家族に会わせるために連れてきたとき、家族が遠慮がちになることを予想するかもしれません。」

分詞構文（現在分詞または過去分詞で始まる）は、文脈によってさまざまな意味になりますが、ここでは条件を表し、"If you are from an Asian family" と同じ意味になります。

その他の意味になる例を挙げると、

a）時を表す場合

Seeing a police car, he ran away. (= When he saw a police car, ...)
「彼はパトカーを見ると、逃げ出した。」

b）原因・理由を表す場合

Being tired, she went to bed early. (= Because she was tired, ...)
「彼女は疲れていたので、早目に就寝した。」

c）付帯状況を表す場合

She said, "Good-bye," <u>smiling at me</u>. (= ...while she was smiling at me.)
「彼女は私に微笑みかけながら「さよなら」と言った。」

d) 結果を表す場合

A big typhoon hit the island, <u>causing great damage</u>. (= ... and it caused great damage.)
「大きな台風がその島を襲い、多大な被害をもたらした。」

4   **Listen to the dialogue and fill in the blanks.**

会話文の音声を聞き、空所に適切な語をいれなさい。

Mary: Hi, Richard. Long time no see. How're you and Keiko doing these days?

Richard: Hi, Mary. It's a long time since we met last summer. So, yeah, I'm well, thank you, and Keiko is busy as usual, working at the bank, doing aerobics, and taking cooking classes. How about you, Mary? How have you and Kenji been lately?

Mary: Well, you know my husband is a system engineer. He often comes home late at night. Sometimes he looks (1.   ) from working such long hours. So, I just keep away from him when he looks tired out.

Richard: Oh, really? But don't you think communication is important for a couple, especially those from different cultures?

Mary: It depends. Of course, language is very important. That's why I started to learn Japanese at the culture center. I was born and (2.   ) in California. I didn't speak Japanese well, and Kenji wasn't good at speaking English when he asked me for a date. Honestly, I was very worried about the (3.   ) (   ) between us.

Richard: Sure, I understand. I felt the same way you did. I come from Boston, while my wife comes from Kyoto. I started from scratch in trying to understand the Japanese way of thinking.

Mary: I see. I'm beginning to realize that what's most important in a relationship is understanding our partners' feelings. That's why if my husband wants to be alone, I give him the time and space to do that.

Richard: Right, I see what you mean. I know Kenji is a very (4.   ) and patient man. I guess he'd occasionally like to have time to think by himself.

Mary:　That's true. One other thing, though—besides our cultural differences, I think our misunderstandings sometimes just come from differences in our personal backgrounds, such as our families, the kinds of places we grew up in, and the different experiences that we've had. Anyway, how about you, Richard? What causes (5.　　　) to fly between you and Keiko?

Richard: Well, Keiko and I often disagree with each other on what to eat, the TV programs we want to watch, and how to spend our free time. Those are probably issues for any couple, I guess.

Mary:　Yes, I agree. So, Richard, I've told you my ideas. Tell me, what are your tips for maintaining good relationships with people from other cultures?

📝 NOTE

tip: 秘訣

---

⑤ What's your opinion?

Mary の問いかけに、自分の考えを述べてみましょう。

Mary: What are your tips for maintaining good relationships with people from other cultures?

You: I think ＿＿＿＿＿ is important because ＿＿＿＿＿＿＿＿＿＿＿＿＿

次の❻ Cultural Information: Do you know? も参考にしてください。

⑥ Cultural Information: Do you know?

異文化理解能力

　1990 年以後、情報通信技術の急速な発展で、経済や社会の活動が、国家

を越えて、地球規模で、さまざまな現象を引き起こしています。このグローバリゼーションに伴い、国を越えて、国籍、民族などの異なる大量の人々が移動・定住し、私たちは、言語、宗教、生活様式等の異なる人々とともに共存し、ともに生きていく多様な多文化時代を迎えています。日本においても、たくさんの海外からの観光客が急増し、国籍の異なる人々による国際結婚の数も 2000 年半ばまで急増してきました。

（八島智子・久保田真弓，2012）

このような時代において、つぎのような異文化理解能力（多文化の人と円滑にコミュニケーションを図っていく能力）を育てる態度が必要です。
1．自分の考えと違っても、「よくない」と思わずに、相手の考え方を理解、尊重する姿勢を持ち相手と話し合いをすることができる。
2．自分の文化中心の見方にとらわれず、相手の文化の観点からも物を眺めてみようとする自分の世界で当たり前となっている常識を見直すことができる。
3．相手の異なる考えや価値観を受けとめるオープンな心がある。
4．自分の文化と異なる違いに否定的になったり、感情的にならずに、まずその判断を保留し、違いが生じた状況を冷静に眺めることができる。
5．相手の違いを受けとめる柔軟な態度がある。

（八代京子・荒木昌子　他，2011）

✒ Related Vocabulary

globalization: グローバリゼーション　international marriage: 国際結婚
intercultural/cross-cultural communication: 異文化コミュニケーション
increase sharply, soar: 急増する　flexible frame of mind: 柔軟な態度　ethnic
group: 民族（集団）　multiculturalism: 多文化主義

CHAPTER 1

Young Japanese Seek K-Pop Stardom in South Korea

オンラインで容易に音楽を視聴・購入することができる現在、海外の音楽を聴く機会も多いかもしれません。世界中の人と触れ合える国境なき音楽の世界を考えてみましょう。
Daniel Megias (iStock by Getty Images)
※写真はイメージです。

The popularity of K-pop has led to a number of young people leaving their home countries and going to South Korea, the center of the K-pop universe. Industry experts estimate there may be up to one million music hopefuls seeking stardom in South Korea. While most of these young men and women are South Koreans, a growing number come from Japan, where K-pop has a huge following.

One person who hopes to become a K-pop star is 17-year-old Yuuka Hasumi. She left her high school in Japan and went to South Korea in hopes of becoming a star performer. Hasumi knew her new life in South Korea would not be easy. She would need to spend long hours working on her voice and dance moves. There would be little time for social activities. This would mean giving up much of her privacy, having no boyfriend, and having little or no use of her smartphone.

The young woman signed up to attend the Acopia School in Seoul, a preparatory school offering young Japanese a shot at K-pop fame. Acopia teaches students K-pop songs and dance moves, as well as the Korean language. Such training programs are the first step for Hasumi and others trying to prepare for an intensely competitive series of auditions. All the music hopefuls dream of getting invited to perform for major talent agencies. In the end, the agencies accept only a small number of "trainees" to shape into possible stars.

Hasumi is one of about 500 Japanese who join the Acopia School each year. The program costs up to $3,000 a month. The cost includes training activities and a place to stay. When students are ready, the school can organize auditions for them with talent agencies. Industry experts say the auditioning process has fueled a

"Korean-wave" of pop culture that has spread worldwide over the past 10 years.

One of the biggest K-pop groups to explode into stardom was the South Korean boy band BTS. "They're nuts about BTS over there in Japan," said Lee Soo-chul, who belongs to the Seoul-Tokyo Forum, a private group that has members from the Japanese and South Korean diplomatic and business communities.

K-pop's huge popularity comes at a time when South Korea and Japan are experiencing difficulties in their relationship. But Lee says K-pop groups and well-known Korean musicians keep performing to large, sell-out crowds throughout Japan. "There is no Korea-Japan animosity there."

16-year-old Rikuya Kawasaki is another Japanese K-pop star hopeful. "I might get criticized for being Japanese, but I want to stand on stage and let South Koreans know that Japanese can be this cool," he told interviewers.

Some Japanese have already made it big in K-pop. The three Japanese members of the girl band TWICE helped make the group a success. TWICE is now the second most popular K-pop band in Japan, after BTS.

Yuuka Hasumi is hopeful that K-pop can be good for relations between the two countries. "It will be great if Japan and South Korea can learn to get along better through music," she said.   (520 words)

🖊 NOTE

K-pop: 韓国 (Korea) のポピュラー音楽　the Acopia School：アコピアスクール　韓国ソウル市にある中高生向けの語学留学、ダンス留学機関　offer ～ a shot：（人）に～の機会を与える　nuts: 狂っている、夢中の　BTS: 2013 年にデビューした男性ヒップホップグループ　sell-out crowds: 満員の観客・聴衆　TWICE: 2015 年に結成された女性アイドルグループ

1　　**How many words do you know?**

次の単語の意味を、右の選択肢から選び記号で答えなさい。

1. explode	(　)	a. 競争力の高い	
2. fuel	(　)	b. 憎悪、激しい嫌悪	
3. band	(　)	c. 審査、オーディション	
4. estimate	(　)	d. ～を加熱させる、～を加速させる	

5. competitive   (   )   e. 大躍進する

6. animosity   (   )   f. 〜だと推定する

7. audition   (   )   g. 演奏したり歌う音楽グループ

2 **Reading Comprehension: True or False**

次の英文が、本文の内容に合っていれば T を、合っていなければ F を（　　）
内に書きなさい。

1. More and more young Japanese are seeking to be K-pop stars in South Korea.

（　　　　）

2. Yuuka Hasumi did not realize she would have a hard life in South Korea
until she arrived in the country.   （　　　　）

3. Students at the Acopia School have a lot to learn before they can attend
auditions.   （　　　　）

4. K-pop groups and the crowds at their concerts in Japan do not have a good
relationship.   （　　　　）

5. Rikuya Kawasaki gave up his dream of becoming a K-pop star because he
was criticized for being Japanese.   （　　　　）

3 **Grammar section**

「動名詞の意味上の主語」

K-pop popularity has led to a number of young people leaving their home
countries and going to South Korea.

「Kポップ人気は多くの若者が祖国を出て韓国へ行くという結果につながっ
た。」

動名詞（〜 ing）の意味上の主語が文全体の主語とは異なる場合には、動名
詞の前に意味上の主語となる名詞（句）か代名詞を置く必要があります。
この意味上の主語は、目的格か所有格の形で置かれます。意味上の主語が名
詞（句）の場合は目的格のもの（そのままの形）で置きますが、代名詞や人
の名前の場合は、所有格または目的格の形にして置きます。

a）名詞（句）が意味上の主語となる場合
　　People were afraid of a comet hitting the earth.

「人々は彗星が地球に衝突することを恐れていた。」
（名詞（句）をそのまま動名詞の前に置く）

ｂ) 代名詞が意味上の主語となる場合

She was afraid of <u>his/him</u> having an accident.

「彼女は彼が事故にあうのではないかと恐れていた。」
（代名詞は所有格または目的格の形で動名詞の前に置く）

4　Listen to the dialogue and fill in the blanks.

会話文の音声を聞き、空所に適切な語をいれなさい。

Lisa:　Hi, Daiki. Are you interested in K-pop? I'm always listening to it these days.

Daiki:　Of course, I'm (1.　　　) about it! I often go to K-pop concerts in Japan. There are (2.　　　) crowds all the time at those shows.

Lisa:　Wow, that's amazing! Did you know that more and more young Japanese are going to Korea, dreaming of being K-pop stars?

Daiki:　Really? Are the auditions tough (3.　　　) there?

Lisa:　Yes, only a few are accepted. The auditioning process has influenced trends in pop culture and the world market. Luckily, auditions are held in Japan, too.

Daiki:　Oh, really? Why is that?

Lisa　Japan is the second (4.　　　) music market, next to the U.S. Surprisingly, some Japanese have become members of popular K-pop bands.

Daiki:　Oh, that's wonderful! I hope that trend will help both countries get along with each other without any (5.　　　).

Lisa:　Yes, that would be absolutely great! So, what do you think about those young Japanese hopefuls?

Lisa の問いかけに、自分の考えを述べてみましょう。

Lisa: What do you think about those young Japanese hopefuls?
You: I think ＿＿＿＿＿＿＿＿＿＿ because ＿＿＿＿＿＿＿＿＿＿＿＿＿＿

次の❻ Cultural Information: Do you know? も参考にしてください。

6　　**Cultural Information: Do you know?**

K-Pop 発祥の歴史

　韓国のポピュラー音楽は、日本のポピュラー音楽と深い関係があります。1980 年代までの韓国歌謡はその特色として、作曲家・演奏家のキル・オギュンがいうように、「伝統的歌謡」、「欧米の影響の下にある歌謡」、日本からの影響を受けた「倭色歌謡」が挙げられます。日本で J-Pop という言葉が使われ始めたのは、1988 年後半からで、この頃から音楽が多様化して、「POP」自身も変化していきます。

　1987 年から 1997 年の間に、韓国社会の活性化とともに、新しい K-Pop の原形が現れました。J-Pop とアメリカンポップの影響を受けながらも、韓国独自の「新しい感覚」が生まれ、アメリカのケーブルステーションや日本型アイドルの「観る音楽」に強く反応した韓国の若者に受け入れられるルックス、歌唱力、パフォーマンスの優れた K-Pop アイドルの歴史が始まりました。

（金成玟，2018）

K-Pop スターになるには

　K-Pop は、2000 年初めに台湾や中国に K-Pop ブームを作り、海外に進出して成功をおさめています。KARA、少女時代、東方神起、BTS，TWICE 等を目指して、明日のスターになるためには、どのようなステップを踏んだらいいのでしょうか。

　韓国では、まずテレビの公開オーディション番組や、事務所のオーディションに応募し、合格しなければなりません。この「厳しいオーディション」に合格すると、事務所に所属し、「練習生」と呼ばれる「アイドル予備軍」と

なります。この予備軍になるだけでも「狭き門」で、激しい競争率です。この間、事務所はダンス、歌のレッスン、食事代、寮費を負担し、惜しみなく明日のスターに投資します。これに答えるように、練習生は長くて7〜9年、平均5年といわれる練習生生活に励みます。1日に10時間以上のレッスンを何年も受けてデビューするので、歌、ダンスとも完成度が高いと評価されています。「ダンス」や、「声の出し方」のレッスンのほか、個人の特性、才能に応じて、オリジナルのトレーニングプログラムがあり、演技、作曲、語学、社会人としてのマナートークなども選択します。

（鄭城尤 〈監修〉・酒井美絵子 〈著〉, 2012）

✎ Related Vocabulary

talented icons: 才能あるアイコン的な存在　Japanese idol: 日本のアイドル
appearance, looks: ルックス　personal characteristics: 人の特性　Japanese
annexation of Korea: 日韓併合　compensate: 〜を賠償する　international
law: 国際法

CHAPTER 03

Malala Yousafzai: Warrior with Words

マララ・ユスフザイさんは、2010年代に世界で最も有名な10代の少女の1人だったといえます。彼女の身に起きたことや世界への影響について思い出してみましょう。

Children's books on Malala Yousafzai

Malala Yousafzai is known for promoting education as a basic right, especially education for women and children. The young Pakistani activist became world famous after she was attacked by a Taliban militant because she expressed support for the education of girls. She has since won awards for her human rights work. In 2014, at the age of 17, she was the youngest person to win the Nobel Peace Prize. She shared the 2014 prize with a child rights campaigner from India. Malala has authored books, and many have been written about her.

Malala has come a long way since her childhood in rural Pakistan. In the year 2007, the influence of the Taliban was growing in Pakistan's Swat Valley. Malala's father owned a school there and supported her writing about life under the Taliban for a British website. Schools for girls were closed, but Malala continued to write and speak publicly about the importance of education for all children, especially girls.

Her life changed forever in 2012, when she was 15 years old. On a ride home from school, a Taliban gunman boarded her bus. He shot Malala and two of her friends. They survived, but Malala's wounds were severe. She was taken to a hospital in Birmingham, England. There, she recovered from a wound to her head and fortunately had no lasting injury to her brain.

Less than a year later, when she turned 16, Malala was at the United Nations in New York, speaking out for education. In her book "Malala Yousafzai, Warrior with Words," writer Karen Leggett Abouraya describes the speech as a turning point.

"And there she was in front of the United Nations. It was a group of young people, and she was speaking on her birthday. 'We will bring change through our voice,' she said. She asked every nation to make it possible for all children to go to school and live in peace. 'Our words can change the world.'"

Jenni L. Walsh, author of the book "She Dared—Malala Yousafzai," continues the story. "Malala wondered out loud: 'How can they stop more than 50,000 girls from going to school in the 21st century?'"

Today, Malala Yousafzai is studying philosophy, politics, and economics at the University of Oxford. She says she fights every day so that all girls will receive 12 years of free, safe, and quality education. (400 words)

✏️ NOTE

Pakistani: パキスタン人（の）　the Nobel Peace Prize: ノーベル平和賞　a Taliban militant: タリバン、イスラム原理主義者の武装集団　board: ～に乗りこむ　shoot (shoot-shot-shot):（銃・弾丸を）発射する・撃つ　lasting injury: 後遺症として残る怪我　Karen Leggett Abouraya: "Malala Yousafzai, Warrior with Words" の作者　Jenni L. Walsh: "She Dared — Malala Yousafzai" の作者

---

1 How many words do you know?

次の単語の意味を、右の選択肢から選び記号で答えなさい。

1. recover	(	)	a.	賞
2. author	(	)	b.	質
3. promote	(	)	c.	(病気などが) 重大な、深刻な
4. severe	(	)	d.	回復する
5. award	(	)	e.	～を促進する
6. quality	(	)	f.	哲学
7. philosophy	(	)	g.	著者

2 Reading Comprehension: True or False

次の英文が、本文の内容に合っていれば T を、合っていなければ F を（　　）内に書きなさい。

1. Malala Yousafzai started her activities to promote girls' education after she was

attacked by a Taliban militant. (   )

2. Malala was the only person who won the Nobel Peace Prize in 2014. (   )

3. Malala's father helped her with her activities. (   )

4. It took many years for Malala to recover from her head injury. (   )

5. In her speech at the United Nations, Malala asked the world to promote education for all children. (   )

3 Grammar section

「不定詞の意味上の主語」

She asked every nation to make it possible for all children to go to school.

「彼女は各国に、すべての子供たちが学校に通うことを可能にするよう要求した。」

1. 不定詞（to + 動詞の原形）の意味上の主語

不定詞の意味上の主語を明示する必要がある場合には、その前に for 〜という形を置いて表します。上の文では「学校に通う」のは「すべての子供たち」であることになります。

for all children to go …
   (S)   (V)

2. 形式目的語／形式主語の it と真の目的語／真の主語

ところで、この文の中程にある it は形式目的語（仮の目的語）で、「『それ』を可能にする」と言っておいて、後から『それ』の指す中身（真の目的語）として意味上の主語をともなった不定詞の部分「すべての子供たちが学校に通うこと」が続いていることになります。

（形式目的語）　　（真の目的語）
make + it + possible + for all children + to go...

このように、「意味上の主語をともなう不定詞」（for all children + to go...）は、形式目的語（仮の目的語）や形式主語（仮の主語）として前に出てきた it の指す中身（真の目的語／真の主語）として使われることが多いです。

形式主語の it の指す中身（真の主語）として意味上の主語をともなう不定詞が使われている例を一つ挙げておきましょう。

（形式主語）　　　　　　　（真の主語）

It was easy for John to pass the entrance exam for this school .

「ジョンがこの学校の入試に合格するのは容易なことだった。」

4 Listen to the dialogue and fill in the blanks.

会話文の音声を聞き、空所に適切な語をいれなさい。

Daichi: Hi, Yuka. I read a book called "I Am Malala" recently. It was a very moving story. Have you ever read it?

Yuka: No, I haven't, but I've heard of Malala. She's a world-famous human rights activist from (1.　　　　　), right? I think she believes in the right to education for women and children, especially for girls.

Daichi: Yes, that's right. When she was 15 she was shot in the head by a Taliban gunman while riding a school bus. Two other girls were shot, too. Since Malala's (2.　　　　) was very serious, she was transferred to a hospital in Birmingham, England. While she was there, she received a huge pile of cards from people all over the world wishing for her recovery. It was a miracle that she (3.　　　　) from her injury.

Yuka: Why did the Taliban attack such a young girl?

Daichi: Malala spoke out in public. She said that girls in Pakistan should be educated at school, just like boys. The Taliban, an Islamic fundamentalist group, didn't like that idea. They believe education for girls isn't necessary. In their view, girls are expected to help with household work and get married at a young age.

Yuka: Oh, I remember reading an article in the newspaper about that. The region Malala lived in was not (4.　　　　) at that time. A lot of people were killed in fights between the government and the Taliban.

Daichi: Yes, it was a very difficult time. Fortunately, Malala survived and in 2014, at the age of 17, she became the youngest person ever to (5.　　　　) the Nobel Peace Prize. I still remember her speech when she accepted the award.

Yuka: What parts made the biggest impression on you?

Daichi: I like two statements. "The pen is mightier than the sword" and "One child, one teacher, one book can change the world." Those words really touched my heart.

Yuka: Oh, I'm impressed by them, too. It's true, education is essential for all children. So, Daiki, in addition to education, what other problems do you think developing countries face?

5 **What's your opinion?**

Yuka の問いかけに、自分の考えを述べてみましょう。

Yuka: What are some problems that developing countries face?
You: I think _____

次の**6**の Cultural Information: Do you know? も参考にしてください。

6 **Cultural Information: Do you know?**

国際ガールズ・デー (International Day of the Girl Child)

　2011 年 12 月、国連総会において 10 月 11 日は「国際ガールズ・デー」と制定されました。女児が受ける不当な差別やその改善について世界中で考えていこうという、国連が新たに制定した国際デーです。世界の国々、特に開発途上国では、女子の多くが、経済的、文化的な理由により学校に通えず、10 代前半で結婚を強制され、貧困のなかで暮らしています。女児の置かれた状況に関心をもち、人権を尊重することを目的として女児の可能性を広げ未来を切り開くための日です。国連児童基金(ユニセフ)も議論に加わりました。
（国際 NGO プラン・インターナショナル）

開発途上国での学校に通えない子どもの割合

　今世界では、6 歳から 17 歳の女子のおよそ 1 億 3,200 万人が学校に通えない現状です。そのうち 75％が 10 代です。就学率は、地域によって格差がみられますが、女子のほうが、男子より低い傾向にあります。低所得国では、初等教育を修了する女子は 3 分の 2 に満たず、前期中等教育（日本では中学校）ではわずかに 3 人に 1 人の割合です。サブサハラアフリカ（サハラ砂漠より南の地域）を初めとする一部の地域では、前期中等教育を修了する女子の割合が平均わずか 40％です。
（UNICEF, 2018）

教育は、悪循環を断ち切る力

　下図の貧困の悪循環を断ち切るには、女子の教育は大変重要です。女子が教育を受け、知識や技術を身に付け、適正な職業に就くことが出来れば、本人だけでなく家族、地域、そして将来生まれる子供にも良い影響をもたらすと考えられます。

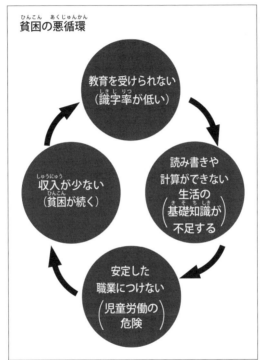

（関橋眞理，2013，汐文社）

✏️ Related Vocabulary

poverty: 貧困　　literacy rate: 識字率　　elementary/primary education: 初等教育　　child labor: 児童労働　　child marriage: 児童婚　　human trafficking: 人身売買　　fair trade: フェアトレード（適正な賃金・適切な労働条件・環境配慮）　　force ～ to... : ～に…することを強制する

CHAPTER

04

Iceland Celebrates 30 Years Since End of Beer Ban

飲酒や喫煙に関するルールは、法律や宗教だけでなく時代によっても変化します。どのような理由や根拠に基づいて変化し、その国の人々はどのように思うのでしょうか。
photo by Delphine

Thirty years ago, Icelanders drank beer legally for the first time in decades. The drink had been outlawed in Iceland for 74 years. All other types of alcohol had remained legal, however. The beer ban finally ended on March 1, 1989. The country recently celebrated the anniversary of the end of its long ban on beer. Fittingly, the celebration is called "Beer Day."

The beer ban was held over from the country's prohibition days, which began in 1915 after the population voted in a referendum to outlaw all alcohol. The ban partly ended just seven years later out of economic need. Spain refused to buy Iceland's largest export, fish, unless Iceland bought Spanish wines.

The prohibition of alcohol ended in another national referendum in 1933, when a very small majority voted to change the law. However, Iceland's parliament decided to continue to ban beer.

Alcohol abuse remains a problem in Iceland. One in 10 Icelandic men over the age of 15 have received treatment for alcohol dependency at least once, the country's leading addiction treatment center, SAA, says.

Most Icelanders agree with strong government restrictions on alcohol sales to reduce alcoholism. All alcohol — including beer — is only sold at government-run stores and is highly taxed. A drinker can also, of course, just go to a bar, where a pint of beer usually costs about 1,100 krona (US 9 dollars, or roughly 1,000 yen).

Icelanders' opinions of beer began changing in the 1970s, when more of them started traveling to sunny European beach resorts and enjoying the drink. The call for beer in their own country became strong. Yet even by 1988, many people were against ending the beer ban, including some politicians.

Steingrimur Sigfusson is parliamentary speaker. He recalls that, at the time, there was a real fear of change. Many thought hundreds of bars would open for beer-drinkers and change society for the worse. Sigfusson himself voted against ending the ban. He still defends the country's restrictive alcohol policies that aim to prevent alcohol abuse and under-age drinking. "The worst-case predictions never came true, but underage drinking did increase," he said.

When the ban finally ended exactly 30 years ago, all four bars in Iceland's capital, Reykjavik, were full of happy drinkers. In one day, Iceland's 260,000 people bought an astounding 340,000 cans of beer at government-run alcohol stores.　(388 words)

✐NOTE

referendum: 国民投票　prohibition: 禁酒・禁酒令　addiction treatment center: （薬物・アルコール）依存症治療センター　SAA: アイスランドの薬物・アルコール依存症患者の更正施設を運営する NGO 組織　a pint of beer: ビール一杯（一パイントはイギリスで約 0.55 リットル）　parliamentary speaker: 議会議長　Reykjavik: アイスランドの首都レイキャビーク

---

1 **How many words do you know?**

次の単語の意味を、右の選択肢から選び記号で答えなさい。

1. decade	（　　）	a. 禁止令
2. alcoholism	（　　）	b. 制限
3. ban	（　　）	c. アルコール依存症
4. outlaw	（　　）	d. 十年間
5. abuse	（　　）	e. 〜を弁護する
6. restriction	（　　）	g. 〜を非合法化する
7. defend	（　　）	f. 乱用

Reading Comprehension: True or False

次の英文が、本文の内容に合っていればTを、合っていなければFを（　　）内に書きなさい。

1. It was illegal to drink any type of alcohol in Iceland for 74 years. （　　）

2. Icelanders could drink Spanish wines legally from 1922 onward. （　　）

3. The ban on beer was lifted after a national referendum in 1933. （　　）

4. Alcoholism is still a major social problem in Iceland. （　　）

5. Sigfusson is one of the politicians who voted in parliament to end the beer ban.

（　　）

Grammar section

Grammar Point　「主語＋動詞＋補語（第2文型）」
Alcohol abuse remains a problem in Iceland.
「アルコールの乱用は、アイスランドでは依然として問題である。」

上の文では、alcohol abuse「アルコールの乱用」が主語、remain「〜のままでいる」が動詞、a problem「問題」が補語となっており、「主語＋動詞＋補語」という形の、一般に「第2文型」と呼ばれる文型になっています。
この文型では主語と補語の間に、ある種のイコールの関係が成り立っています。（上の例では alcohol abuse = a problem ）また、補語になり得るものは名詞（句）または形容詞です。
この文型で最も多く用いられる動詞は be 動詞であり、たとえば次のような文が典型例です。

His father is a famous actor.
「彼の父親は有名な俳優です。」　(his father = a famous actor)

ただ、最初の例文のように一般動詞が用いられる場合もかなりありますが、この文型でよく用いられる一般動詞には、remain「〜のままでいる」のほか、become「〜になる」、get「〜（の状態）になる」、turn「〜に変わる」、look「〜のように見える」、sound「〜に聞こえる」、feel「〜のように感じる」、taste「〜な味がする」などがあります。下にいくつか例文を挙げておきます。

The leaves on the trees turn red and yellow in autumn.
「秋には木々の葉が赤や黄色に変わる。」

She looked tired yesterday.
「彼女は昨日疲れているように見えた。」

The tea tasted bitter.
「そのお茶は苦い味がした。」

4 Listen to the dialogue and fill in the blanks.

会話文の音声を聞き、空所に適切な語をいれなさい。

Daichi: Hi, Yuka. A friend of mine told me that she enjoyed visiting Iceland last March. She recommended traveling there.

Yuka: Oh, Iceland's near Britain, isn't it?

Daichi: No, no! Not Ireland — *Iceland*. You know, the place near the Arctic Ocean.

Yuka: Oh, sorry. You mean the country near Greenland? How's the weather in Iceland? The name of the country (1.   ) me of cold weather.

Daichi: Well, in fact, Iceland has a fairly warm climate all year round because of the Gulf Stream. So the names of the two countries are (2.   ) up. Actually, Iceland is green and Greenland is icy.

Yuka: That's interesting. Do you know any good sightseeing spots in Iceland?

Daichi: Let's see, I've been reading a guidebook that introduces day tours in Reykjavik, the (3.   ) of Iceland. There are a lot of historical and geological places of interest in the city and around that area.

Yuka: Oh, really? What kind of tours do they offer?

Daichi: Well, there's a volcano tour where you can travel by jeep to see traces of lava flows, and another tour where you can go to the top of a breathtaking glacier in a snowmobile.

Yuka: Amazing! Those both sound like spectacular adventures! What about the historical sites?

Daichi: Yes. One is Hofdi House in Reykjavik. An important summit meeting between former U.S. President Ronald Reagan and former U.S.S.R. Secretary General Mikhail Gorbachev took place there in 1986.

Yuka: Oh, I read about that in my history class. What else in Iceland are you interested in?

Daichi: I'm really interested in bathing in the milky blue water at the Blue Lagoon and taking a spa (4.   ) there. I'm sure that would be very relaxing. You know, there are more than 200 active volcanoes in Iceland. People can visit hot-water spas all year round.

Yuka: There must be some traditional foods. What do they have there?

Daichi: Iceland has an abundance of seafood, such as salmon, lobster, cod, crab, and other kinds of shellfish. They often serve their delicious seafood with a pint of beer. Icelanders really enjoy drinking beer since the end of the beer (5.   ).

Yuka: Oh, my mouth is watering. You should definitely go there!

Daichi: What would you like to do in Iceland if you could go, Yuka?

⑤ What's your opinion?

Daichi の問いかけに、自分の考えを述べてみましょう。

Daichi: What would you like to do in Iceland if you could go, Yuka?

You: If I could go, I'd _____.

次の ❻ Cultural Information: Do you know? も参考にしてください。

⑥ Cultural Information: Do you know?

アイスランドの自然

　アイスランドはノルウェーとグリーンランドにはさまれた北大西洋のほぼ中央に位置し、200 以上の火山と全国土の約 11％の氷河を持ち「火と氷の島」と呼ばれています。北極海のすぐ南に位置しますが、沿岸を流れる暖かいメキシコ暖流のおかげで、緯度の割には、冬は穏やかで、夏は涼しい気候です。面積は、北海道よりやや大きく 10.3 万平方キロメートル、人口密度は少なく、人口は 34 万 8,580 人（アイスランド統計局, 2017 年 12 月）で、そのうち南西部の首都レイキャビクと周囲の市を含めた首都圏で全人口の約 60％の人が住んでいます。

　中央部は巨大な氷河のある山岳地帯と高原台地で、人の居住しない地帯で、

人が住むのは、首都レイキャビクを中心とした沿岸地帯で、美しい緑におおわれた牧草地・多くの活火山・豊かな温泉とフィヨルドがみられます。豊富な地熱資源から得た地熱発電や、地熱による給湯を利用した地域・家庭の暖房で見られるように、自然の力を最大限に利用し、汚染されていないので、空気が澄んで新鮮です。また緯度が低く、白夜の季節が短いので、通常オーロラの季節が8カ月間の長さで、美しいオーロラを楽しむ旅を楽しめます。
（株式会社ヴァイキング，2009；外務省アイスランド共和国基礎データ，2018）

（アイスランドの観光地　海外旅行準備室 Iceland-kankobunnka.jp）

✎ Related Vocabulary

the Arctic Ocean: 北極海　glacier: 氷河　lava flow: 溶岩流　hot spring, spa: 温泉　geothermal power generation: 地熱発電　abstain from alcohol: 禁酒する　alcohol percentage: アルコール度数　liquor store: 酒屋

Naomi Osaka Sponsor Drops Ad after Criticism

「他の人と異なる」ということは、肯定的にも否定的にも捉えられることがあります。自分と相手との「違い」にどのように接していくべきか考えながら読んでみましょう。
Matthew Stockman by Getty Images

Japanese tennis star Naomi Osaka says she hopes the companies she represents will talk with her about how to present her image in future advertisements. Osaka was asked about criticism of her sponsor, Nissin Foods Holdings. The company produced an animated advertisement that showed Osaka with skin that looked lighter than her real skin color.

Critics said the ad does not represent Osaka's darker skin or her biracial background. Osaka was born in Japan to a Japanese mother and a Haitian American father. Nissin has since removed the advertisement from YouTube.

"I've talked to them. They've apologized," Osaka said. "I'm tan. It's pretty obvious." Osaka said she did not think the company's aim was to "whitewash" her. But she added, "I definitely think that the next time they try to portray me...they should talk to me about it."

Daisuke Okabayashi is a spokesman for Nissin Foods Holdings. He said Thursday the company did not mean to disrespect Osaka's biracial background. The ad also showed Kei Nishikori, another Japanese tennis star, with lighter skin. Okabayashi said Osaka's representative approved the ad but later asked to have it taken down. He said the company continues to support Osaka and does not want the issue to become a distraction.

It is not the first time that a Japanese company has faced criticism for how it deals with issues of race and nationality. Baye McNeil is an American who has lived in Japan for more than 10 years. He wrote an opinion article for The Japan Times, a popular English-language newspaper. McNeil wrote, "I found a whitewashed representation of Osaka that could've easily been based on a TV personality like Becky or Rola."

McNeil told the Associated Press that Japanese companies need to become more inclusive if they hope to appeal to a worldwide market. "They are not thinking on that level," McNeil said. "It may be painful, but Japan is going through growing pains regarding diversity right now." (325 words)

✐ NOTE

sponsor: スポンサー、広告主　Nissin Foods Holdings: 日清食品ホールディングズ animated advertisement: 広告動画　ad: 広告　tan: 黄褐色の　whitewash: 肌の 色を白く調整する、ホワイトウオッシュ　biracial background: 2つの人種をもつ背 景　distraction: 障害　Becky or Rola: タレントのベッキーとローラ　inclusive: すべてを含んだ、包括的な

---

① How many words do you know?

次の単語の意味を、右の選択肢から選び記号で答えなさい。

1. represent	( )	a.	あきらかな
2. criticism	( )	b.	肌
3. skin	( )	c.	〜を描く
4. portray	( )	d.	批判
5. obvious	( )	e.	多様性
6. apologize	( )	f.	〜の代表となる・〜を表す
7. diversity	( )	g.	あやまる

---

② Reading Comprehension: True or False

次の英文が、本文の内容に合っていればTを、合っていなければFを（　　）内に書きなさい。

1. Nissin Foods Holdings used Naomi Osaka's photo for its advertisement.
（　　）

2. Nissin was criticized because Osaka's skin color in their advertisement was

not true to life. (　　　)

3. Nissin continued using the advertisement even after it was criticized.

(　　　)

4. According to a spokesman for Nissin, the company wants to maintain their good relationship with Osaka. (　　　)

5. According to one American writer, Japanese companies need to be more sensitive to differences among people. (　　　)

3 | **Grammar section**

「使役動詞としての have」

Osaka's representative approved the ad but later asked to <u>have it taken down</u>.
「大坂の代理人はその広告を承認したが、後にそれを削除してもらうよう依頼した。」

have は使役動詞として「〜させる」「〜してもらう」という意味を表すことができますが、形としては次の 2 通りの場合があります。

a) have + 目的語 + 動詞の原形

He <u>had</u> <u>his son</u> <u>wash</u> his car.
「彼は自分の息子に車を洗わせた（洗ってもらった）。」

この場合、目的語は通例人を表すものになり、目的語と動詞の原形との間には、「〜（人）が・・・する」という能動態的な意味関係が成り立ちます。（上の文では「息子が車を洗う」(his son washes his car) という意味関係になります。）

b) have + 目的語 + 動詞の過去分詞形

He <u>had</u> <u>his car</u> <u>washed</u> by his son.
「彼は自分の息子に車を洗わせた（洗ってもらった）。」

この形では、目的語に物である his car が来て、目的語と動詞の過去分詞形との間には「〜（物）が・・・される」という受動態的な意味関係が成り立ちます。（上の文では「車が息子によって洗われる」(his car is washed by his son) という意味関係になりますが、文全体としては　a) の文と同じことを言っていることになります。）

最初に挙げた例文では、have + <u>it (the ad)</u> + <u>taken down</u>...
　　　　　　　　　　　　　　（目的語）　　（過去分詞形）

という形になっており、「その広告が削除される」(the ad is taken down) という受動態的な意味関係が成り立っていることになります。

4　Listen to the dialogue and fill in the blanks.

会話文の音声を聞き、空所に適切な語をいれなさい。

Daichi: Do you like tennis, Yuka?

Yuka:　Yes, I often watch it on TV. I'm a big fan of Naomi Osaka!

Daichi: Isn't she the Japanese player who won Grand Slam singles titles at the US Open and the Australian Open?

Yuka:　Yes, that's right. She's the first (1.　　　　) tennis player to win a Grand Slam. Her (2.　　　　) play and cute personality attract a lot of people.

Daichi: I heard that many people were thrilled by her performance in the final against Serena Williams at the 2018 US Open. By the way, do you know about her (3.　　　　) so-called whitewashing controversy?

Yuka:　No. What happened?

Daichi: Nissin Foods Holdings showed Naomi with much lighter skin color in their (4.　　　　) commercial on YouTube.

Yuka:　Really? What did she say?

Daichi: She said her skin is naturally tan and that next time the sponsor should talk to her first before creating an ad with her in it. They apologized, and the ad was taken off of YouTube.

Yuka:　Her (5.　　　　) race background of Japanese and Haitian American should be respected. Why did such a thing happen in Japan?

✏ NOTE

the US Open: 全米オープン　全米テニス協会主催・運営

5   What's your opinion?

Yuka の問いかけに、自分の考えを述べてみましょう。

Yuka: Why did such a thing happen in Japan?

You: I think _____

次の ❻ Cultural Information: Do you know? も参考にしてください。

6   Cultural Information: Do you know?

ハーフは英語？

　私たちの日常生活では、テレビや新聞などのメディアを初め、日常会話においても、英語だと思われそうなカタカナ表記の言葉であふれています。しかし、それらの言葉の中には、海外では通じない和製英語 (Japanese English) が多く見受けられます。たとえば、ガソリンスタンド、サラリーマン、ペーパードライバーなどです。ハーフと言う言葉もそうです。よく両親のどちらかが、海外からの出身者である場合、その子供を「ハーフ」と呼びますが、これは正しい英語表現ではありません。

　よく使う表現として、"mixed" という言葉があります。もし日本人とスウェーデン人の子供の場合は、

　"I'm mixed race. My mother is Japanese and my father is Swedish."

　"I'm biracial, Japanese and Swedish."

と言います。もし "half" という言葉を使う場合には、具体的に次のように言います。

　"I'm half Japanese and half Swedish."

　それでは、複数の background を持つ人は,"What am I ?" という問いに、どのような答えをだすのでしょうか。自分のアイデンティティを考える場合、お父さんもお母さんもそして生まれ育った場所や環境もすべて大切で、ひとつに絞られないかもしれません。結局、自分が好む表現を選び、表わせばいいのではないでしょうか。

世界で活躍する日本出身の 'mixed' のスポーツ選手

　最近、両親の国籍が違う日本出身のスポーツ選手が世界で注目されていま

す。本文で紹介されたテニスの大坂なおみ選手はお父さんがハイチ系アメリカ人、お母さんが日本人、男子バスケットボールで NBA のワシントン・ウィザーズで活躍する八村塁選手は、お父さんがベナン人でお母さんが日本人、陸上競技 100m、200m で優れた記録保持者で、2017 年からフロリダ大学に進学しているサニブラウン・アブデル・ハキーム選手は、お父さんがガーナ人、お母さんが日本人です。

> ## ✍ Related Vocabulary
>
> ethnic background: 民族的背景　nationality: 国籍　race: 人種　mixed: 混血の　inherit: (性格などを) 受け継ぐ　heredity: 遺伝　play on a global stage: 国際的に活躍する

CHAPTER 06

Two Musicians Play Across Cultures

「音楽に国境はない」とは、先に読んだポップミュージックだけでなく、伝統的な音楽にも該当します。日本の伝統音楽でもそうなのか、考えながら読んでみましょう。

Masood Omari and Abigail Adams Greenway both love the tabla, a musical instrument from South Asia consisting of two differently pitched drums. They formed a duo called Tabla for Two and play at embassy and museum events, universities, and at the Tablasphere, a colorful room in Greenway's house, for invited guests.

It is unusual for two tabla players to play together, and this gives the duo a modern sound.

"We play new music for the New World, as we call it. It's our signature music and it is composed by Masood," Greenway explained. They also play classical Indian and traditional music from Afghanistan and India.

"I grew up listening to classical music and American jazz," Greenway said. "My father was a classical violinist."

She became interested in the tabla when she first heard the music of India. "I heard the music and I just thought, this is the most amazing instrument I've ever heard," she said, adding, "They say that when the student is ready, the teacher appears."

Greenway met Omari eight years ago at a store that sells Afghan goods. He had fled Afghanistan when he was 15 and settled in Pakistan, where he studied tabla for ten years before coming to the United States in 2002.

"I realized that he was this amazing tabla player and I asked for lessons. I didn't know at the time where this was going. All I knew is that I had a huge desire and a force pushing me to learn to play the instrument."

After spending two years studying hard and playing together, the two musicians formed Tabla for Two. Greenway feels she does not have problems being accepted as a woman playing Afghan music.

"I am clearly an American female and I am playing their music. It's a coming together of cultures," she said. "When I play this music the Afghan people are accepting me."

In fact, both musicians feel like ambassadors for Afghan music. "I believe that I have an important role, playing and preserving the music of my country, Afghanistan, and sharing it with the world," Omari says. (349 words)

✎ NOTE

tabla: タブラー、北インドの伝統太鼓の一種、タブラー（高音用の小さい太鼓）とバーヤ（低音用の大きい太鼓）の２種類を組み合わせ、指を駆使して、多彩な音を奏でる pitched drum: 音程を調整したドラム　duo: デュオ、２人組　Tablasphere：タブラーの間、タブラー演奏用の部屋　signature music：独自の音楽

---

1 How many words do you know?

次の単語の意味を、右の選択肢から選び記号で答えなさい。

1. embassy	( )	a. 大使
2. flee	( )	b. 〜を作曲する
3. ambassador	( )	c. 楽器
4. preserve	( )	d. 大使館
5. compose	( )	e. 素晴らしい、驚くほどの
6. amazing	( )	f. 〜を保護・保存する
7. instrument	( )	g. 〜から逃げる、避難する

2 Reading Comprehension: True or False

次の英文が、本文の内容に合っていればTを、合っていなければFを（　　）内に書きなさい。

1. Omari and Greenway play their music in public places.　　　　（　　）

2. Tabla players commonly play together in duos. (　　　)

3. Before discovering Indian music, Greenway enjoyed listening to classical music and jazz. (　　　)

4. Omari taught Greenway how to play the tabla. (　　　)

5. Afghan people did not like to hear their music played by Greenway.

(　　　)

3 | **Grammar section**

「最上級＋完了形」

This is <u>the most amazing</u> instrument (that) I <u>have</u> ever <u>heard</u>.

「これは今まで私が（その音色を）聞いた中で、いちばんすばらしい楽器だ。」

<u>形容詞の最上級（the ＋ 形容詞 -est / the ＋ most ＋ 形容詞）＋ 名詞</u>という形の後に、<u>現在完了形（have (has) ＋ 過去分詞）</u>を使った節が続くと、「今まで・・・ した中で最も〜な ---」という意味になります。（ちなみに、この場合の現在完了形は「・・・ したことがある」という経験を表す用法です。）

最上級 ＋ 名詞と、現在完了形を使った節の間には、文法的には関係代名詞の that が入りますが、しばしば省略されます。また、have (has) と過去分詞の間には、「今までに」という意味を強調する ever がよく使われます。

a) 最上級 ＋ 現在完了形の例：

Venice is <u>the most beautiful city</u> (that) I <u>have</u> ever <u>visited</u>.

「ベニスは私が今まで訪れた中で最も美しい都市だ。」

ところで、最上級が使われている主節（前半の部分）の時制が「過去時制」である場合には、後ろの節では<u>過去完了形（had ＋ 過去分詞）</u>が使われ、「それまで ・・・ した中で最も〜な ---」という意味になります。」

b) 最上級 ＋ 過去完了形の例：

Venice was <u>the most beautiful city</u> (that) he <u>had</u> ever <u>visited</u>.

「ベニスは彼がそれまで訪れた中で最も美しい都市だった。」

Listen to the dialogue and fill in the blanks.

会話文の音声を聞き、空所に適切な語をいれなさい。

Daichi: Hi, Yuka. I went to a concert last night. It was awesome!

Yuka: Really? What kind of concert?

Daichi: Richard Mingus and his band. He's a pretty famous rock musician.

Yuka: What (1.   ) does he play?

Daichi: He sings and plays the keyboard, and his band play guitars and drums. I was very (2.   ) by their performance and their improvising skills.

Yuka: Does he write his own songs?

Daichi: Oh yes! He's (3.   ) a huge variety, from children's songs to love songs. It's (4.   ) to think he has recorded 900 songs. You might have heard some on TV. He sings about love and peace, but he is best known for his songs about nature. His music relaxes me and makes me happy.

Yuka: Those feelings are precious and (5.   ) these days, so I'd love to listen to his music. How often do you go to concerts, Daichi?

Daichi: Once a month. I really love live music. Yuka, do you play a musical (6.   )?

Yuka: Yes, the saxophone. I used to be a member of the brass band club in my junior high school days. I remember tuning the sax before practice was not easy for me. We practiced every weekday.

Daichi: Every weekday? Wow, that's real dedication for you! Yuka, what music do you like?

What's your opinion?

Daichi の問いかけに、自分の考えを述べてみましょう。

Daichi: What kind of music do you like?

You: I like _____ because _____

次の **6** Cultural Information: Do you know? も参考にしてください。

Cultural Information: Do you know?

民族楽器ーアジア編ー

　民族楽器は、太古から、宗教および儀式で神や霊を呼び出すものとして、また、社会生活においては集いや人々の出会いにおいて、対話と物語を作り出すものとして演奏されてきました。「人間が音を出す目的で作ったたくさんの道具」という共通の概念を持った楽器（musical instrument）は幾世代にもわたって形を変えながら、文化の推移を刻み込んできました。

　チベットの砂時計型の太鼓ダマルは、本体に結び付けられた紐の先に小さな玉がついて、この太鼓を振ることにより、紐の端の小球が膜面をうち、音を出します。人間の頭蓋骨からできた場合は、頭蓋太鼓とも呼ばれます。胴には宗教的な場面が描かれ、ふつうチベットの仏教の儀式や寺院で使用されます。

　韓国の十二弦琴カヤグムは、日本の琴に似た形をしていますが、琴は13弦でつめを使って演奏するのに対し、カヤグムは、12弦でつめを使わずに演奏します。弦は絹の糸からできていて、12個の可動柱によって音の高さを調整し、豊かなヴィブラートや音の高低の変化を含むさまざまな音響効果を作り上げることができます。

　中国のフィドル（擦弦楽器）の二胡は、2本の弦を間に挟んだ弓でひいて演奏します。シンプルな外見にもかかわらず、表情豊かな音を出すことができ、中国の古典や民衆曲の合奏に欠かせません。即興で長い旋律を奏でることもでき、独創楽器としても用いられています。（図1）

　遊牧民のリュート（撥弦楽器）や、フィドル（擦弦楽器）は、単純で適当な自然素材で作られ、弦は動物の腸や、植物の繊維などで作られています。モンゴルの遊牧民ハルハ族の馬頭琴は、装飾が施された糸蔵も、馬の毛を使った弦も、弓や胴の装飾にいたるまですべてが馬に関係しこの楽器は、馬が大事な遊牧社会で生まれたものだということを示しています。（図2）

jxfzsy (iStock by Getty Images)

図1

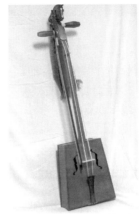

kazukied2 / PIXTA(ピクスタ)

図2

📝 Related Vocabulary

folk music, ethnic music 民族音楽　　ceremony: 儀式　　Tibetan Buddhism: チベット仏教　　drum: 太鼓　　string: 弦　　bow: 弓　　Mongolia: モンゴル　　pastoral society: 遊牧社会

CHAPTER 07

Native American Mascots, Redface, and Logos Are Slowly Disappearing

少数派や弱い立場にあるグループの存在は無視されるべきではありません。一方で、存在を強調すれば解決するわけでもありません。互いの立場の背景や現状を考えてみましょう。

photo by Charlie Lyons-Pardue

Native Americans, Nicholet Deschine Parkhurst and John Little, are both unhappy about how indigenous people in the U.S. are often represented as relics of the past in contemporary America.

"When you're viewed in that way, as only existing in the past, as the 'frozen Indian' found in museums, it makes it harder for voices of leaders in our communities to actually be heard, and it's easier for people to ignore us," Nicholet said.

In 2017, John made a documentary, "More Than a Word", about the Washington Redskins, an American football team, and its chosen name. In it, fans explain why they think the team name honors Native Americans. These fans paint their faces, perform their versions of a Native American dance or war cry, and wear fake headdresses.

These are examples of "redface", acting like a Native American in clothing, speech, or by painting your face. Unlike "blackface", which is now taboo, redface is not often discussed. But to many Native Americans, the sight of sports fans wearing feathered headdresses is highly insulting. The headwear is historically a sign of great honor and respect, earned by tribal chiefs.

Experts say that redface gets less attention than blackface for a number of reasons. One is that Native Americans make up less than 2% of the United States' population. African Americans, by comparison, make up about 13%. Another is the set of deep-rooted but mistaken ideas about American history many European Americans have.

Philip J. Deloria is a Harvard University history professor. He says most people think those old images, largely based on 19th-century Plains Indians, represent who Native Americans were and still are.

"There's a big, long, complicated history to this that's really deep in American culture. It's every bit as deep as blackface minstrelsy and slavery. It's just out there, but we've kind of forgotten about it."

Although changes have been slow, there have been some positive signs. The Cleveland Indians baseball team, for example, has new clothing for players that does not include the image of "Chief Wahoo", a Native American face shown in bright red and wearing one feather. Also, the U.S. Lacrosse Association plans to remove offensive Native American mascots and signs from all events that it organizes. (369 words)

✎ NOTE

the Washington Redskins: ワシントン・レッドスキンズ　ワシントン D.C. 都市圏に本拠地をもつプロアメリカンフットボールリーグ　fake headdress: にせものの羽根飾りがついた冠・頭飾り　Plains Indians: 平原インディアン　北アメリカ大陸中部の平原地域に住む先住民の総称　blackface minstrelsy: ミンストレル・ショー　白人（1840年代から黒人も）が顔を黒く塗り、踊り・音楽・寸劇をするアメリカ合衆国のショー　1850年代から1890年代に盛んに演じられた　Chief Wahoo:「ワフー酋長」　2018年まで使用されたアメリカ合衆国のプロ野球チーム「クリーブランド・インディアンス」のマスコットキャラクター　the U.S. Lacrosse Association: 全米ラクロス協会

1　How many words do you know?

次の単語の意味を、右の選択肢から選び記号で答えなさい。

1. relic　　　　　　（　　　）　　a. 部族の
2. indigenous　　　（　　　）　　b. ～を取り去る、～を撤廃する
3. contemporary　（　　　）　　c. 先住の、土着の
4. insult　　　　　（　　　）　　d. 侮辱的な、無礼な
5. tribal　　　　　（　　　）　　e. 現代の、同時代の
6. remove　　　　（　　　）　　f. 遺物・遺跡
7. offensive　　　（　　　）　　g. ～を侮辱する

Reading Comprehension: True or False

次の英文が、本文の内容に合っていれば T を、合っていなければ F を（　　）
内に書きなさい。

1. Parkhurst and Little are members of Native American communities.
   （　　　）

2. Native American people are proud that a famous football team is named
   the Washington Redskins. （　　　）

3. The number of Native Americans in the United States is larger than that of
   African Americans. （　　　）

4. Nicholet Deschine Parkhurst wants Native Americans to be portrayed in a
   more modern way. （　　　）

5. Nowadays, Native American images are seen less often in the world of
   American sport than they were before. （　　　）

3

Grammar section

「関係代名詞の制限的用法と非制限的用法」
Unlike "blackface", which is now taboo, redface is not often discussed.
「"ブラックフェイス" というもの、それは今ではタブーとなっているが、そ
れとは異なりレッドフェイスはあまり議論されることがない。」

関係代名詞と、その前の先行詞の間にカンマ（,）が入ると、「非制限的用法」
という使い方になります。この場合、関係代名詞の節は先行詞についての情
報を補足する働きをして、「（ところで）それは／その人は・・・なのだが」
という意味になります。

a) 関係代名詞の非制限的用法の例：
   She has a son, who is a professional football player.
   「彼女には息子が一人いるが、その息子はプロのフットボール選手なので
   す。」

上の例では、「彼女には一人だけ息子がいる」、と言っておいて、その一人息
子について補足的に「その息子はプロのフットボール選手だ」という情報を
あとから付け加えていることになります。

また、非制限的用法の関係代名詞の節は、いちばん上の例のように文の途中に入ることもよくありますが、その場合には前と後ろにカンマが入って挿入句的に用いられます。

b) 関係代名詞の制限的用法の例：

She has a son <u>who is a professional football player</u>.
「彼女にはプロのフットボール選手である息子が一人いる。」

先行詞と関係代名詞の間にカンマが入らない場合は「制限的用法」という使い方になり、関係代名詞の節が後ろから先行詞の意味を限定します。上の例では、彼女には「プロのフットボール選手 である息子」が一人いることになりますが、ほかにも違う職業についている息子がいる可能性があります。

4 **Listen to the dialogue and fill in the blanks.**

会話文の音声を聞き、空所に適切な語をいれなさい。

Daichi: Hi, Yuka! I've got an American history exam next Thursday. It's a challenging but rewarding subject. I'm really interested in the (1.   ) people of the U.S.

Yuka: You mean the people (2.   ) to the country before Columbus arrived in America?

Daichi: That's right. Professor Maeda recommended us to watch the Hollywood movie "Dances with Wolves" starring Kevin Costner. He told us it would help us understand the life of the Sioux (3.   ) living in South Dakota during the Civil War.

Yuka: Interesting! I'd like to watch it, too.

Daichi: The Sioux hunted buffalo and were one of the most powerful (4.   ) Indian tribes. The movie is set in the 1860s and describes the deep relationship between a Sioux tribe and an American soldier.

Yuka: I'm curious about Native American history. Where do they live now?

Daichi: That's a good question. At the end of the 19th century, after a long fight against the federal government, they were forced by law to live on reservations. They ended up losing most of their original land.

Yuka: That's terrible! What's it like for young people living on the reservations today?

Daichi: Most Native Americans are poor, especially on the reservations, and the assimilation policy from the end of the 19th century still casts a shadow. Young people have a lot of problems there. Although they can get an education at boarding schools outside the reservations, they can't make good use of what they learn when they go back as there are few job opportunities.

Yuka: How are they regarded in American society?

Daichi: Discrimination is a problem. More and more young Native Americans are suffering from alcoholism, drug addiction, and (5.　　　　) addiction. The number committing suicide is going up, you know.

Yuka: Those are very serious problems. I think young people should live with hope for the future. How can the situation be improved?

📝 NOTE

Dances with Wolves: 1990 年度制作　複数のオスカー賞を受賞したアメリカ映画
assimilation policy: 19 世紀末に始まった同化政策　子供を寄宿舎に住ませ、部族の言葉や宗教を否定し、主流社会の英語教育、キリスト教教育、職業訓練等を施す政策

5　What's your opinion?

Yuka の問いかけに、自分の考えを述べてみましょう。

Yuka: How can the situation of Native Americans be improved?

You: I think ＿＿＿＿＿ is important because ＿＿＿＿＿＿＿＿＿＿＿＿

次の ❻ Cultural Information: Do you know? も参考にしてください。

6　Cultural Information: Do you know?

スポーツの世界におけるアメリカ先住民のイメージ乱用

　スポーツ界でも、アメリカ先住民のイメージを乱用し、部族固有の文化や名前をチームロゴのイメージに使用したり、マスコットにしたりしているこ

とが、先住民の人権回復が叫ばれた1960年代ごろから、とくに問題視されてきた。アメリカ先住民を象徴する色は「赤」で、1960年代から70年代にかけて先住民自身もこの「赤」を使用し、レッド・パワー・ムーブメントを展開した。

　なぜ赤のイメージが使われるかについては、酔っぱらったインディアンの顔が赤かったからという、偏見に満ちた説もあれば、肌の色が赤みがかっているからという説や、儀式や戦闘の際に顔を赤く塗っていたからという説もある。また白人の所有する黒人奴隷と区別するために、先住民みずからが赤い人種というアイデンティティをつくったともいわれている。

　イリノイ大学の平原部族の酋長のような恰好をした応援団長「イリュニック」は、歪んだストレオタイプを拡大すると認められ、2007年2月にイリノイ大学はその応援スタイルを自粛する決定を下した。オハイオ州のメジャー・リーグのチーム、クリーブランド・インディアンズも、先住民にちなんだ名称について、先住民団体から批判されている。選手の被る帽子とユニホームにも縫い付けられたチームロゴの「チーフ・ワフー」は赤っぽい肌で、頭に羽飾りをつけ、鼻が大きく、不敵で漫画チックな笑みを浮かべ、アメリカ先住民を侮蔑する人種差別だと抗議がなされ、2019年からは使用を中止された。

（鎌田　遵，2009）

✎ Related Vocabulary

tribe: 部族　　reservation: 居留地　　democratic: 民主的　　chief: 酋長　　protest against 〜：〜に抗議する　　hierarchy: 階級制度・ヒエラルキー　　invasion: 侵略 attachment to the land: 土地への愛着

米国における先住民の権利擁護のために集まったアメリカ先住民族の人たち

Native nations gather to stand up for Indigenous rights in the US. © Amanda J. Mason / Greenpeace

Singapore Grows More with Less on "Sky Farms"

「空中農園」と言うと、ノンフィクションの世界のように思われるかもしれません。これはもう実現している現代の様子です。農業は今後さらにどんな発展を遂げるのでしょうか。
psisa / PIXTA（ピクスタ）

Big changes in agriculture are taking place in Singapore. The tiny southeast Asian country aims to increase its food production by growing vegetables on top of office buildings. It has also set up tiered fish farms and is using laboratories to grow shrimp, a popular treat.

With just 1% of its land area of 724 square kilometers devoted to agriculture, Singapore can produce only about 10% of its food. But as climate change and population growth threaten food supplies, it wants to raise that to 30% by the year 2030, under a plan known as "30-by-30." The problem is space.

"Whenever I talk about food security in Singapore, I tell folks don't think land, think space, because you can go upwards," said Paul Teng, a professor of agriculture at Nanyang Technological University.

There are more than 30 vertical farms in Singapore — farms that grow upwards, not outwards. The number of so-called "sky farms" has doubled over the past three years. Sustenir Agriculture is one of these businesses. Its hydroponic farm grows non-native foods like kale, cherry tomatoes, and strawberries inside buildings under artificial lighting. Then it sells the produce to local supermarkets and online stores. Another forward-thinking company, Apollo Aquaculture Group, is building a highly-automated, eight-story fish farm that will allow them to achieve a 20-fold increase in production.

"It is too unpredictable to do things now in the traditional way," said Apollo chief Eric Ng. In recent years, there have been problems with algae blooms killing off farmers' fish.

Not everyone thinks the new technology is best. Egg farmer William Ho says the government should not depend so much on agriculture technology businesses.

"Many of them have failed. That's why I'm always asking the government, why don't you invest in us old-timers? We are more practical," he said.

Professor Paul Teng said an issue for urban farmers is that the high cost of the technology makes their products too pricey for many people.

One new business is Shiok Meats. It aims to be the world's first to sell shrimp grown from cells in a laboratory. The process involves cells grown in a nutrient solution in tanks. After four to six weeks, the fluid is removed, leaving small pieces of shrimp. (374 words)

✏ NOTE

tiered: 層になった　(be) devoted to: 〜にあてる、ささげる　folks: (一般の) 人々
vertical farm: 垂直農園　Sustenir Agriculture: ハイテク技術を駆使し都市型農業を実施しているシンガポールの会社　hydroponic farm: 水栽培農場　forward-thinking: (考え方が) 先進的な　nutrient solution: 栄養溶液　20-fold: 20 倍の
algae bloom: 藻類の発生　Shiok Meats: 研究者のSandhya Sriam 氏と Ka Yi Ling 氏により起業されたシンガポールの会社　エビ等の人工製品の開発を進めている

---

1 How many words do you know?

次の単語の意味を、右の選択肢から選び記号で答えなさい。

1. agriculture	(　)	a. 楽しみ、ごちそう
2. laboratory	(　)	b. 生産物（野菜・果物など）
3. security	(　)	c. 都会の
4. artificial	(　)	d. 実験室
5. produce	(　)	e. 安全
6. urban	(　)	f. 農業
7. treat	(　)	g. 人工的な

Reading Comprehension: True or False

次の英文が、本文の内容に合っていれば T を、合っていなければ F を（　　）
内に書きなさい。

1. Singapore produces enough food for its population. （　　）

2. The number of "sky farms" is increasing because there is not enough space
   for agriculture in Singapore. （　　）

3. Sustenir Agriculture exports all its produce to other countries. （　　）

4. Apollo Aquaculture Group grows fish in a traditional way. （　　）

5. Food produced in sky farms is expensive. （　　）

3 Grammar section

「付帯状況を表す with」

With just 1% of its land area of 724 square kilometers devoted to agriculture,
Singapore can produce only about 10% of its food.
「724 平方キロの国土のうちたった 1 パーセントが農業にあてられているな
かで、シンガポールはその食料の約 10 パーセントしか生産できていない。」

with + 目的語 + 補語（形容詞／分詞／前置詞句）という形で、
「〜が・・・という状況をともなって」という意味（付帯状況）を表します。

a) 補語に形容詞が用いられる場合
　　Don't speak with your mouth full.
　　「口いっぱいにものをほおばったままでしゃべるな。」

b) 補語に分詞（現在分詞／過去分詞）が用いられる場合
　　He came along with his dog following him.
　　「彼は犬を連れてやってきた。」（現在分詞の例）

　　She sat on the bench with her legs crossed.
　　「彼女は足を組んでベンチに座っていた。」（過去分詞の例）

c) 補語に前置詞句が用いられる場合
　　He stood there with a pipe in his mouth.
　　「彼はパイプを口にくわえてそこに立っていた。」

Listen to the dialogue and fill in the blanks.

会話文の音声を聞き、空所に適切な語をいれなさい。

Daichi: Hi, Yuka. How have you been?

Yuka: Great! I just got back from Singapore.

Daichi: Oh, that's wonderful. Tell me about it.

Yuka: Well, Singapore is a great place for shopping and eating out. There are lots of large shopping malls, swanky shops, and amazing restaurants.

Daichi: What did you buy?

Yuka: Just a few souvenirs. I was mainly window shopping. Singapore is rather expensive!

Daichi: How did you get around?

Yuka: By train. It's a (1.　　　　) country, and you can get from one end to the other in no time.

Daichi: I heard almost everyone lives in cities in Singapore.

Yuka: That's right, it's almost all (2.　　　　). But that's what makes the Singapore Botanic Gardens so special.

Daichi: Ah, that's a World Heritage Site, isn't it? Did you go?

Yuka: Yes I did, and you're right, it's a World Heritage Site, Singapore's only one. It's a huge garden and it took me a long time to walk around.

Daichi: What did you see there?

Yuka: Oh, many things. The best for me were the beautiful orchids. So many different colors!

Daichi: What else did you do in Singapore?

Yuka: I went on a (3.　　　　) tour. That was really interesting. There is very little space for (4.　　　　) in Singapore, so they have to think of new ways to farm. One idea is growing vegetables in (5.　　　　) to prevent disease. Another is building farms vertically, like a multi-story building. They build upwards because they can't build outwards.

Daichi: Impressive! I'd like to go one day. What more do you know about Singapore?

Daichi の問いかけに、自分の考えを述べてみましょう。

Daichi: What more do you know about Singapore?

You: _____

次の❻ Cultural Information: Do you know? も参考にしてください。

6   **Cultural Information: Do you know?**

都市型農業を実施しているシンガポールのハイテク産業

　最近シンガポールは農産品の国内生産を推進しており、国の土地は狭いが技術革新が進み、垂直農業や、狭いスペースを有効に活用する水耕栽培も可能になった。環境センサー、モバイルコンピューティング、衛星、イメージング、ドローン、ワイヤレス通信などを活用した効果的な農業を可能にする技術もどんどん開発されている。

　国内生産に寄与している会社の一つが日本の電気メーカーのパナソニックで、2015 年には 1,154 平方メートルの野菜工場を開設している。その他、国内のベンチャー企業として、Sustenir Agriculture は LED ライト、エアコンダクト、自動灌漑システムを使った水耕栽培を行い、Archisen は IoT(Internet of Things) を使って、屋内農業向けのシステム開発をしている。

（碇　知子，2017）

✎ Related Vocabulary

organic farm: 有機栽培　　pesticide: 殺虫剤　　preservative: 保存剤
hydroponics: 水耕栽培　　grocery: 食料雑貨店、食料品　　population density:
人口密度　　drone: ドローン　　satellite:（人工）衛星

Kenya's Deaf Rugby Team Hopes to Match National Team's Success

障害を持つ人たちのスポーツには、どのような難しさ・工夫があるのでしょうか。聴覚障害の場合を例に、読んで考えてみましょう。

Rugby is one of Kenya's most popular sports, and the country's national team has played in the World Cup. Inspired by the national team's success, members of Kenya's deaf community launched a deaf rugby team last year. The team, which has been training for just more than a year now, has big dreams for the future.

Every Sunday, Martin Kasuivya begins his journey to the rugby pitch with a rush of excitement in his eyes. He had played football (soccer) as a child, but had never played rugby until a year ago, when officials of the newly formed Kenya Deaf Rugby Association came to his church.

Martin was born deaf and has largely remained within the deaf community in Kenya. He spoke to the writers of this story through a sign language interpreter.

"Before, when I was growing up, there was no deaf rugby, but people like to join new things, so I thought, let me go with a new thing," he said.

At the pitch, about an hour's commute from his house, Martin joins 16 other players for practice. This has become the team's weekly Sunday afternoon routine. The players in Nairobi haven't played a game yet and don't have a sponsor. They make do with what they have: one ball, which they all chipped in to buy, and mismatched secondhand uniforms. There's no whistle when they play. In a professional deaf rugby match, the referee waves a white flag to draw the attention of the players.

The team's coach, Brennan Rashid, communicates with players through sign language. Unlike the players, Rashid is not deaf. He says that despite their lack of playing experience, the team is getting better.

"I have seen progress; I have seen them going places step by step, getting a proper understanding of the game, and that is the best thing I can give them," he said.

Despite the various hardships, Kasuivya and the other players have big dreams, like competing in the Deaf Olympics, which comes up next in 2021. South Africa, Australia, Canada, and England will all be sending teams. Kasuivya says the team has one goal: win the gold. (357 words)

📝 NOTE

launch: 〜を始める　a rush of excitement: 胸の高鳴り　sign language: 手話　make do with:（手近なもので）間に合わせる、済ます　chip in: 〜のために寄付する、お金を出し合う　Kenya Deaf Rugby Association: ケニア聴覚者障害ラグビー協会　the Deaf Olympics: デフリンピック　4 年に 1 度、世界規模で行われる聴覚障害者のための総合スポーツ競技大会

---

❶ How many words do you know?

次の単語の意味を、右の選択肢から選び記号で答えなさい。

1. deaf	(　　)	a. 苦難
2. inspire	(　　)	b. 競う
3. routine	(　　)	c. 〜を元気づける
4. interpreter	(　　)	d. 通勤
5. commute	(　　)	e. 通訳
6. compete	(　　)	f. 日常の仕事・日課
7. hardship	(　　)	g. 耳が聞こえない、耳の不自由な

❷ Reading Comprehension: True or False

次の英文が、本文の内容に合っていれば T を、合っていなければ F を（　　）内に書きなさい。

1. Kenya's deaf rugby team was formed after its national rugby team played in the World Cup. (　　)

2. Martin Kasuivya lost his hearing as a child. (　　)

3. Martin and his teammates practice once a week. ( )

4. The reason Martin's team plays without a whistle is because they do not have enough money to buy one. ( )

5. Kasuivya and his teammates hope to play games with teams from other countries. ( )

③ Grammar section

「過去完了形」（had ＋動詞の過去分詞形）
He <u>had played</u> football (soccer) as a child, but <u>had</u> never <u>played</u> rugby until a year ago.
「彼は子供の頃サッカーをしたことはあったが、一年前までラグビーをしたことはなかった。」

過去完了形（had ＋ 動詞の過去分詞形）は、基本的に過去のある時点を基準として、その前に何かが起こっていたことを表します。

過去完了形の表す出来事
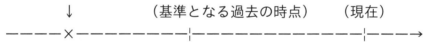
    ↓   （基準となる過去の時点）   （現在）

上の文では 1 年前を基準にして、それ以前にサッカーをしたことはあったが、ラグビーをしたことはなかったと言っていることになります。

過去完了形は、現在完了形（have + 動詞の過去分詞形）と同様に、場合によって「完了・結果」、「経験」、「継続」などを表します。

a)「完了・結果」を表す過去完了形 （あるときまでに〜してしまっていた）
The train <u>had</u> already <u>left</u> when he arrived at the station.
「彼が駅に着いたときには、列車はすでに出発してしまっていた。」

b)「経験」を表す過去完了形 （あるときまでに〜したことがあった）
Taro <u>had climbed</u> Mt. Fuji twice before he was twenty years old.
「太郎は 20 歳になる前に 2 度富士山に登ったことがあった。」

（最初に挙げた例文も、「経験」を表す例になっています。）

c)「継続」を表す過去完了形 （あるときまでずっと〜していた）
Kate <u>had lived</u> in Australia for five years before she came to Japan.

「ケイトは日本に来る前に5年間オーストラリアに住んでいた。」

4 Listen to the dialogue and fill in the blanks.

会話文の音声を聞き、空所に適切な語をいれなさい。

Daichi: Hi, Yuka. Do you know what the Paralympic Games are?

Yuka: You mean like the Olympics, but for athletes with disabilities?

Daichi: Yes, that's right. Did you know the Paralympic Games have been held (1.   ) after the Olympic Games since the 1988 Summer Olympic Games in Seoul, Korea? There have been both Winter and Summer Paralympic Games since then.

Yuka: So it all started over 30 years ago?

Daichi: Well, the origins of the Paralympics date back to 1948. A group of soldiers injured in World War II were rehabilitating at a British hospital, and a doctor at the hospital organized a sporting event for them on the same day the official Games in London started. Now it has developed into the largest and most (2.   ) international sporting event for people with disabilities.

Yuka: I saw wheelchair rugby on TV once. The players were (3.   ) just like professionals, to the best of their ability.

Daichi: Well, strong will and courage are important to the IPC, together with (4.   ) and justice. They make much of these four values.

Yuka: That's good to hear; they are necessary qualities in our lives, I think. By the way, are there any events for (5.   ) people at the Paralympics?

Daichi: No, there aren't, but there is a special event called the Deaflympics for (6.   ) athletes.

Yuka: Oh, I see. I'd like to watch that, too. How many events in the summer or winter Paralympic Games can you name?

✎ NOTE

IPC: International Paralympic Committee 国際パラリンピック委員会

What's your opinion?

Yuka の問いかけに、自分の考えを述べてみましょう。

Yuka: How many events in the summer or winter Paralympic Games can you name?

You: I know a few. For example, _____ .

次の ❻ Cultural Information: Do you know? も参考にしてください。

Cultural Information: Do you know?

手話（Sign language）

　手話はろう者、耳の聞こえない人の表情や手の動きなどが文法化されてできた言語。世界共通ではなく、地球上に 200 以上あるといわれ、それぞれの国、社会で異なる。代表的な手話に、アメリカの ASL・イギリスの BSL・フランスの FSL (LSF) 等がある。

　学校では、手話で教育する手話法と、ろう児に発音を教え、相手の口の形を読み取らせる口話法の 2 つの教育法の間に長年の論争があったが、近年は、手話言語学の成果などにより、手話は単なるジェスチャーではなく、内部に規則的な構造を持つ言語であるという認識が世界中で広がり、日本においても 2000 年代以後、日本手話が、完全な言語であるとの認識が広がっている。

（斉藤道雄，2016）

ケニアのスポーツ：アスリート養成

　世界のマラソンランナーのトップランキングを見ると、男性の世界歴代 10 傑のうちケニア人が 9 名、エチオピア人が 1 名である。（2011 年 IAAF 国際陸連データ参照）そのケニアには独特なキャンプという養成スタイルがある。多数の一流選手を輩出しているリフトバレー州の 3 か所を紹介する。

　ひとつめは、カプサイト村にある世界でもっとも標高が高い（2800 メートル）altitude training camp（高地トレーニングキャンプ）。ふたつめは、カレンジンの村イテンにあるミッション系の男子高校セントパトリック。ケニアでも特別な陸上の名門校だ。3 つめは、エリート養成所として世界的に有名なアディダスキャンプ。

3つの養成所は、それぞれ違った特色があるが、共通していることは選手が全員世界の舞台で活躍すること、そして結果を出すことができると信じていることだ。信じるだけでは強くなれないが、信じないと強くなれないということも事実だ。信じることが人間の能力の限界を向上させるのだろう。信じた人間を集団養成しているケニアの陸上界は、これからもきっと世界の記録を塗り替えていくだろう。

（石川和博，2012）

✏️ Related Vocabulary

a person with a disability or disabilities/ a disabled person: 身体障害者
athlete: 運動選手　　event: 種目　　ASL: American Sign Language
BSL: British Sign Language　　FSL: French Sign Language　　gesture: ジェスチャー
archery: アーチェリー　　athletics: 陸上競技　　judo: 柔道　　table tennis: 卓球
sitting volleyball: 床に座った姿勢で行うバレーボール　　wheelchair tennis: 車いすテニス

10

"No Handshake? No Kiss?" Greetings in the Age of Coronavirus

新型コロナ流行後、皆さんの周りではどのような変化がありましたか。新しい生活様式のなかで、世界中のコミュニケーションはどう変化しているのでしょうか。
filadendron (iStock by Getty Images)

Every culture has some sort of person-to-person greeting, but these greetings are different all over the world. In some countries, such as the United States, handshakes and hugs are the norm. In many European cultures, kisses on the cheek or "air kisses" near the cheeks are the thing to do when greeting people. And if you play on a sports team, high fives may be the greeting, no matter what your cultural background is. These are our traditions during normal times.

Now, however, because of the coronavirus pandemic, health officials all over the world are urging people to practice social distancing to control the spread of the disease. In these new circumstances, how have person-to-person greetings changed?

Zheng Yu Wen is a television host for Voice of America's China service. Her job involves contact with many on-air guests. So, she says she has changed her guest greeting policy. "Starting today I am telling all my guests who appear in the studio that we don't shake hands anymore. We do elbow touching or foot tapping instead."

Besides the elbow touch and foot tap, there are other ways to greet people without touching at all. Many Asian cultures already use non-contact greetings. Consequently, people in this part of the world may have an easier time avoiding person-to-person contact. In Japan, for example, a bow with both hands kept down to the sides is a traditional greeting.

In Europe, kissing is a common way to greet people. People in France and other parts of Europe often use two kisses, one on each cheek or in the air near the cheeks, as a greeting. People in Switzerland give three kisses.

Now, however, health officials in Switzerland and France have advised people to stop the traditional kiss greeting. Also, the Italian government has completely banned kissing during greetings in an effort to stop the spread of the coronavirus.

This is not the first time a government has made lip contact between people forbidden. In 1439, kissing was temporarily banned in England during ceremonies involving King Henry VI. This was to avoid endangering the King's life during the Plague. Kissing in public was also banned and punishable by death in Naples, Italy around 1562. The reason? To stop the spread of disease. (398 words)

✎ NOTE

handshake: 握手　high five: ハイタッチ　air kiss:（口をすぼめた）キスのまね　social distancing: 人との距離をとること　coronavirus pandemic: 世界的に感染が拡大する新型コロナウイルス　elbow touching: ひじに触れること　foot tapping: 相手と足先を軽くぶつけ合うこと　forbidden: 禁止される　the Plague: ペスト、14 世紀中頃にヨーロッパに広がり、数百年にわたり、世界に複数回大流行した伝染病

1　How many words do you know?

次の単語の意味を、右の選択肢から選び記号で答えなさい。

1. norm	(　　)	a. 罰すべき
2. circumstance	(　　)	b. 儀式
3. bow	(　　)	c. ～に勧告する
4. urge (urging)	(　　)	d. 状況
5. temporarily	(　　)	e. お辞儀
6. ceremony	(　　)	f. 一時的に
7. punishable	(　　)	g. 規範

2　Reading Comprehension: True or False

次の英文が、本文の内容に合っていれば T を、合っていなければ F を（　　）内に書きなさい。

1. European people changed their greeting to "air kisses" because of the

coronavirus pandemic. (　　　)

2. Zheng Yu Wen thinks elbow touching and foot tapping are safer than handshakes. (　　　)

3. It is harder to avoid person-to-person contact in Asian countries when greeting than in the Western countries. (　　　)

4. There are some differences from country to country in the way people use kisses as greetings. (　　　)

5. Historically, Italy is the only country that banned kissing in the past. (　　　)

3 Grammar section

「譲歩の副詞節を導く表現」

If you play on a sports team, high fives may be the greeting, <u>no matter what</u> your cultural background is.

「もしあなたがスポーツチームでプレイしているなら、あなたの文化的背景がどんなものであろうとも、ハイタッチが挨拶になっているかもしれない。」

上の文のように、<u>no matter what</u> +S+V… は譲歩を表す副詞節となり、「何が・・・であろうとも」「何を・・・しようとも」といった意味を表します。

<u>No matter what</u> he says, no one will believe him.
「彼が何を言おうとも、誰も彼を信じないだろう。」

また、no matter what は、whatever で置き換えることも可能で、上の例文は次のように書き換えられます。
<u>Whatever</u> he says, no one will believe him.

同様に譲歩を表す副詞節の表現に、
<u>no matter how</u> + 形容詞／副詞 + S +V… があり、「どんなに・・・しようとも」といった意味を表します。

<u>No matter how</u> hard you try, it is difficult to solve the problem.
「あなたがどんなに懸命に努力しようとも、その問題を解決するのは困難だ。」

また、no matter how は however で置き換えることが可能で、上の文は次のように書き換えられます。
<u>However</u> hard you try, it is difficult to solve the problem.

4 Listen to the dialogue and fill in the blanks.

会話文の音声を聞き、空所に適切な語をいれなさい。

Mika:　What are you doing, Daichi?

Daichi:　I'm preparing a presentation for my seminar tomorrow.

Mika:　Really? What are you going to talk about?

Daichi:　The idea of personal space in the U.S.　We're studying nonverbal (1.　　　　　) across cultures in our class.

Mika:　That sounds interesting. The trip you made to Portland last year should give you some good ideas for your presentation.

Daichi:　Yes, indeed. North Americans keep more personal space than Latin Americans in everyday (2.　　　　　) situations. In fact, I was surprised to see people in the U.S. maintaining a distance between themselves and others while waiting in line at the store.

Mika:　Why do they do that?

Daichi:　I read that it's due to their individualistic culture.　They want to preserve their own private zone, and they expect others to respect their personal boundaries.

Mika:　Oh, I see.　We tend to stand in line close to the people in front of us. At least, that's how it was before the coronavirus (3.　　　　　). Standing close is now forbidden, of course.

Daichi:　I'll give you another example, Mika.　Do you apologize when you happen to touch someone's (4.　　　　　) or some other part of the body when passing on the street?

Mika:　No, not if they're strangers.

Daichi:　Americans will say, "I'm sorry," even to people they don't know.　It's because of the same reason.　Personal space is very important to them.

Mika:　Thanks, Daichi, that's really interesting. I learned that Japan and the U.S. have different ideas about personal space and contact with strangers. Still, I wonder if what you said is true in every case. Japanese might sometimes prefer more space, (5.　　　　　) on the situation.

Daichi:　You're right, Mika. Considering the situation is very important when

we try to understand the way people behave. I'll include that point in
my presentation.

Mika: Daichi, what are some other examples of nonverbal communication
across cultures?

5 What's your opinion?

Mika の問いかけに、自分の考えを述べてみよう。

Mika: What are some other examples of nonverbal communication across
cultures?

You: I think _____ .

次の **❻** Cultural Information: Do you know? も参考にしてください。

6 Cultural Information: Do you know?

ペスト (plague)

　ペストは、ペスト菌による感染症です。　歴史上何度も大規模な波が人類を襲っています。

　14 世紀のヨーロッパの流行では、人口の 3 分の 1 以上がペストによって失われ、皮膚が黒くなる特徴的な症状から「黒死病（Black Death）」と恐れられました。　ペストは現代も世界各地で発生しています。

感染経路は、ネズミなどの野生動物や家畜に寄生するノミが体内にペスト菌を持っていて、このノミに刺されたり、ノミによってペスト菌に感染した動物の体液、血液に触れることによって人に感染します。　またペスト患者の体液や血液に触れたり、肺ペスト患者の近くにいるだけでもペストに感染することがあります。ペストには、感染経路の違いから、腺ペスト、敗血症ペスト、肺ペストの 3 つがあります。

（名古屋検疫所）

非言語コミュニケーション

　非言語コミュニケーションとは、言葉によらない伝達手段を意味します。これはさらに音声が入る場合（vocal）と音声によらない場合（non-vocal）でわけると 4 項目に分類されます。

1. 音声が入る場合 (vocal)：
- パラ言語学： 話し手の声の高さ、声の大きさ、話す速度、間の取り方、声の質、声の表情など。

2. 音声が入らない場合 (nonvocal):
- 身体動作学： 身振り手振り、ジェスチャー、顔の表情、視線の向け方、ふれあいなど
- 近接空間学： 空間や場のとらえかた、縄張り意識、座席の占め方、相手との距離の取り方、列の並べ方など。
- 時間概念学： 時間（遅刻厳禁、時間厳守、スケジュール厳守など）に対するとらえかた、時間概念など。

身体的動作は「ボディ・ランゲージ」といわれるように、手や顔やそのほかの体の部分を使って、自分の意志やメッセージを表します。ジェスチャー（手振り）も、この中に含まれます。異なる文化の人たちで、よく話題にされ、気がつきやすいのが「挨拶」です。非言語コミュニケーションは、文化を越えて共通に使えるものと、そうでないものがあり、誤解や衝突の原因にもなりますので、海外に行く前に事前によく調べておくことが必要です。

Come Here　こっちに来て！

日本では「こっちに来て」と人を呼ぶ時に片手を顔の高さや頭上に上げて招きます。日本人にとって「自分のほうに招く」手先の動きにその意味があるのに対し、アメリカ人は相手方向の手先の動きを見て「あっちへ行って」や「バイバイ」と言う意味に取ります

本来は勝利の意味

日本でもよく使うVサインには手の平を相手に向ける「表サイン」と手の甲を向ける「裏サイン」があり、「裏がえしVサイン」は、イギリス諸島などでは相手を侮辱することになるので、注意が必要です。

（東山安子，2020）

✏ Related Vocabulary

nonverbal communication: 非言語コミュニケーション　gesture: 身振り　personal space: 対人距離　clash of cultures: 文化の衝突　contagious disease:（接触）伝染病　fatality rate: 致死率　be infected: 感染する

11

Cameroon's Palm Tree Worms: Forest Food to Plated Delicacy

苦手な食べ物はありますか。苦手な理由には、味や食感…といろいろな要因が考えられます。「昆虫を食べること」に抵抗があるとすれば、それは何故なのでしょうか。

Eating insects may be unthinkable in your country, but Cameroon's forest tribes have long depended on them to supplement their diets. The palm weevil grub, a fat worm found in palm trees, is such a popular source of protein that it has squirmed out of the forests and onto the plates at popular restaurants, in Cameroon's capital, Yaoundé.

At Le Cercle Municipal restaurant, Chef Emile Engoulou cooks palm weevil grubs to create dishes of international standard. Engoulou says they are the best source of protein, and we have not yet discovered all the nutritional benefits people can get by eating palm tree worms.

For those used to eating meat and fish, finding worms on their dinner plate can be a shock. But the palm weevil grub can also be a pleasant surprise for many consumers, like Paul Ndom. He says the service at Le Cercle Municipal is excellent, the food well-prepared and people are enjoying it. He says he hasn't seen this way of cooking before, but that it is great.

The high demand from chefs, however, has led to a shortage of palm weevil grubs. In fact, the growing popularity of the grub in Cameroon, Chef Engoulou says, has made it several times more expensive than beef. "When we do gastronomy in Cameroon, we need authentic, natural, organic, and precious ingredients. I often like to say that the palm tree worm is the equivalent in Africa of caviar in Europe," he said.

The value placed on the palm weevil grub has not been lost on villagers like Valentin Bidja, who sees the rise in demand as an opportunity for people in rural areas. He used to gather the grubs in the forest but now raises them at home in his village. Not having to go looking for them is less stressful, less tiring, less time-consuming, and more profitable.

People already eat the palm weevil in other African countries, as well as in South America and Southeast Asia. Only time will tell if it climbs onto menus in Europe and beyond. (352 words)

📝 NOTE

Cameroon：カメルーン　中部アフリカにある共和国　首都はヤウンデ（Yaoundé）
palm tree: ヤシの木　palm weevil grub: ヤシオオオサゾウムシの幼虫
squirm：もぞもぞ動く　caviar：キャビア、チョウザメの卵の塩づけ
time-consuming: 時間のかかる

ヤシオオオサゾウムシの幼虫
Luigi Barraco

ヤシオオオサゾウムシ
Noblevmy at Malayalam Wikipedia

1 　How many words do you know?

次の単語の意味を、右の選択肢から選び記号で答えなさい。

1. worm	(　　)	a.	本物の
2. supplement	(　　)	b.	(地域固有の) 調理法
3. ingredient	(　　)	c.	同等のもの
4. nutritional	(　　)	d.	材料
5. gastronomy	(　　)	e.	足のない虫
6. authentic	(　　)	f.	栄養の
7. equivalent	(　　)	g.	～を補う

Reading Comprehension: True or False

次の英文が、本文の内容に合っていればTを、合っていなければFを（　　　）
内に書きなさい。

1. In Cameroon only people living in forests eat palm weevil grubs.　（　　　）

2. Paul Ndom likes the way Chef Emile Engoulou cooks palm weevil grubs.
　　　　　　　　　　　　　　　　　　　　　　　　　　　　　　　（　　　）

3. The price of palm weevil grubs in Cameroon has risen because of their
　popularity.　　　　　　　　　　　　　　　　　　　　　　　（　　　）

4. Caviar is becoming more popular than palm weevil grubs in Cameroon.
　　　　　　　　　　　　　　　　　　　　　　　　　　　　　　　（　　　）

5. Valentin Bidja has changed the way he gets palm weevil grubs.　（　　　）

3

Grammar section

「動名詞」

Eating insects may be unthinkable in your country.
「昆虫を食べることはあなたの国では考えられないことかもしれません。」

上の文では、動詞 eat に -ing が付いて動名詞となり、後ろの目的語 insects
とともに「昆虫を食べること」という一つの名詞句を形成し、それが文全体
の主語となっています。

動名詞は元の動詞の意味を保ったまま「～すること」という意味になり、文
法的には名詞の性質を持つことになります。また、形は現在分詞と同じにな
りますが、別のものです。
上の文では動名詞を核とする名詞句が文の主語になっていますが、目的語や
補語になることもできます。

We enjoyed playing billiards.
「私たちはビリヤードをして（することを）楽しんだ。」（目的語になる場合）
My uncle's hobby is collecting stamps.
「私の叔父の趣味は切手を集めることです。」　　　　　　（補語になる場合）

また、動名詞を否定する場合には、直前に not を置きます。

<u>Not having to go looking for them</u> is less stressful.

「それら（ヤシオオオサゾウムシの幼虫）を探しに行かずに済むことは、よりストレスがかからない。」

上の例では、have to ~「～しなければならない」の have が動名詞になり、さらにそれを not で否定して「～しないで済むこと」となっています。

---

④　Listen to the dialogue and fill in the blanks.

会話文の音声を聞き、空所に適切な語をいれなさい。

Daiki:　Hi, Lisa! I saw a TV program about eating insects last week. The show said it's a good way to solve the global food crisis.

Lisa:　What? Eating insects? It makes me feel (1.　　　　　) just thinking about it.

Daiki:　Well, you may not know that about 100 million people are suffering from hunger now because of poverty, especially in Asian and African countries. This problem will be more serious when the world population reaches over 9.1 billion in 2050.

Lisa:　Yeah, I know. But what (2.　　　　　) does eating insects give us?

Daiki:　Insects are rich in (3.　　　　　), carbohydrates, fats, and minerals, and can be substitutes for meat and fish. They are an eco-friendly option as they don't give off greenhouse gas like cows.

Lisa:　Oh, eating them is good for the environment, then?

Daiki:　You said it. But it's not only that: it's much easier to (4.　　　　　) and farm insects than animals. It makes economic sense. They'll definitely become a sustainable food in the future.

Lisa:　Not in Japan!

Daiki:　Don't be so sure. My grandma told me rice grasshoppers and silk worm pupae were eaten in some areas when she was a little girl.

Lisa:　Really? What about today?

Daiki:　Well, we don't eat insects anymore, but they form part of the traditional diet in some Southeast Asian and African countries such as Thailand, Cambodia, Cameroon, and Uganda.

Lisa:　Which insects do they eat?

Daiki:　Well, for example, the grubs of the African palm weevil are eaten by forest (5.   ) in Cameroon.

Lisa: I wonder how grubs taste.

Daiki: I hear they are very tasty. These grubs are starting to be farmed commercially by the forest communities there.

Lisa: That's a good idea. It not only helps solve the food crisis but also generates income.

Daiki: Absolutely!

Lisa: Do you think eating insects will catch on?

Daiki: Well, it will be difficult for some people to overcome the cultural and psychological barriers to eating insects. What do you think, Lisa?

5 What's your opinion?

Daiki の問いかけに、自分の考えを述べてみましょう。

Daiki: What do you think about eating insects?

You: I think ＿＿＿＿＿＿ because ＿＿＿＿＿＿＿＿＿＿＿＿

次の ❻ Cultural Information: Do you know? も参考にしてください。

6 Cultural Information: Do you know?

昆虫食 (Insect Food)

虫食文化圏

　一般に、ほとんどの虫食文化圏は、東南アジア、サハラ以南のアフリカのような熱帯や亜熱帯にある地帯で、逆に昆虫を食べない文化圏は、ヨーロッパ、ロシア、北アメリカ北部のような温帯にある地帯です。アフリカではシロアリ、モバネワーム、バッタ食、南北アメリカでは甲虫食などの伝統があります。たとえば、東アフリカのウガンダの農村地帯では家族でシロアリを食用に集め、生計を得ています。タイ、ラオス、カンボジアでは、タガメを焼いたり揚げたりして食べています。今後、昆虫食の関心が高まって、北米、ヨーロッパ、東南アジア、アフリカの家族経営の家族・農家と採集する人たちを結ぶ全世界的なネットワークが形成される日がくるのでしょうか。

昆虫の種類

　昆虫食で人気があるのは、チョウや蛾の幼虫、ハチ、バッタ、イナゴ、コオロギ、等です。幼虫としては、蜂の巣に寄生しているワックスワーム（別名ハニーワーム、ハチノスツヅリガの幼虫）、バンブーワーム（タケツトガの幼虫）、ミールワーム（ゴミムシダマシ科の甲虫の幼虫）などがよく知られています。

昆虫食を提唱している人々は、どうしてみんな、昆虫をもっと食べないのかと主張する期待の声が挙がっています。しかしその反面、昆虫の栄養源に関するさらに十分な研究と情報の必要性、技術的・科学的な問題の解決を挙げる声もあります。文化的・倫理的な問題や心理的な心の問題も考慮すべきだという意見もあります。

　今後、いつか、近所のスーパーマーケットで、ポテトチップスの横に、バーベキュー味のコオロギの袋や塩味のキリギリスの袋が置いてあるような時代が訪れるのでしょうか。

　　　　（デイビッド・ウォルトナー＝テーブズ＜著＞・片岡夏実＜訳＞，2019）

✎ **Related Vocabulary**

sustainable food: 持続可能な食料　　nutritional value: 栄養価　　efficient: 効率のよい　　farming: 養殖　　the temperate zone: 温帯　　bug-hunting: 昆虫採集
termite: しろあり

CHAPTER 12

Maz Jobrani: Building Cultural Bridges, One Laugh at a Time

日本の芸能に「漫才」があるように、英語圏にも「スタンドアップコメディ」というジャンルがあります。形式は違えども、舞台に立つコメディアンの目的は同じだといえそうです。

Maz Jobrani feels happy when people laugh at his jokes.

"It's a good feeling because then you realize that it's working, it's relating. The worst feeling is when you're doing stand-up and for whatever reason there is a crowd that doesn't relate to you. Those are the nights when you think to yourself, 'Wow, I can't wait to get off the stage.' But when they get you, it's a great feeling and it's probably one of the reasons you stay up there. It's this drug that keeps feeding you. It's kind of like what I would assume surfing could be because every laugh is like a wave. You want to catch that wave and ride it out until the next laugh comes. So whether it's doing stand-up comedy or putting on a movie, your goal as a comedian is to make people laugh."

Jobrani is no ordinary comedian. He was born in Iran's capital, Tehran, but came to the U.S. when he was six years old, just before the Iranian revolution in 1979. He and his parents moved to California, where he attended school. Jobrani tried a conventional career path, studying political science in college, and even started a Ph.D. program at UCLA. But the comedy of Eddie Murphy was a more powerful influence.

"The reason I'm a comedian is because I'm a fan of comedy. I think what inspired that was Eddie Murphy. When I was younger I used to love watching comedy and discovered Eddie Murphy by watching 'Saturday Night Live.' From there I just wanted to be like Eddie Murphy."

Now as a full-time comedian Maz Jobrani uses comedy to bridge the cultural divide caused by Islamic extremism. His performances both ridicule that extremism and challenge American stereotypes of Muslims. His recent movie, "Jimmy Vestvood: Amerikan Hero", playfully makes fun of American preconceptions of the Middle East.

"I feel that this comedy does have a message, it has a message of peace, it has a message of diplomacy. More importantly, it has a message of showing Iranians in a very different light from how we're used to seeing them. I show them in a fun light. I show them in a light that I don't think most Americans are used to seeing." (379 words)

📝 NOTE

stand-up comedy: コメディアンが一人で舞台に立ち客席の笑いをとるコメディスタイル　put on a movie: 映画に出演する　UCLA: カリファオルニア大学ロサンゼルス校　Eddie Murphy: アメリカを代表するコメディアン・俳優・歌手　Saturday Night Live :『サタデー・ナイト・ライブ』　アメリカの NBC で 1975 年より毎週土曜日に生放送される公開コメディバラエティ番組　Islamic extremism: イスラム過激主義　Muslim: イスラム教徒　Jimmy Vestvood: Amerikan Hero : 2014 年に制作されたコメディ映画　Maz Jobrani が Amir Ohebsion と脚本を担当し、映画主演した

---

1 How many words do you know?

次の単語の意味を、右の選択肢から選び記号で答えなさい。

1. assume	(　　)	a. 外交的手腕
2. stereotype	(　　)	b. 先入観
3. conventional	(　　)	c. 演技、上演、演技表現
4. performance	(　　)	d. ～をあざ笑う
5. ridicule	(　　)	e. 型にはまった
6. preconception	(　　)	f. 固定観念
7. diplomacy	(　　)	g. ～と想定する

2 Reading Comprehension: True or False

次の英文が、本文の内容に合っていれば T を、合っていなければ F を（　　　）

内に書きなさい。

1. Maz Jobrani is a professional surfer as well as a comedian.   (　　　)

2. Jobrani was educated in the US.   (　　　)

3. Jobrani always wanted to be a full-time comedian.   (　　　)

4. Jobrani is an Islamic extremist.   (　　　)

5. Jobrani hopes his movie will change the way American people view Iranians.   (　　　)

3 Grammar section

「関係副詞」

He and his parents moved to California <u>where</u> he attended school.
「彼と両親は、彼が就学することになるカリフォルニアへと移住した。」

関係副詞 where は、場所を表す先行詞の後に続いて、それを説明する節を作ります。（上の例では「カリフォルニア」という場所について、その後彼が就学した場所であることを説明しています。）

関係副詞には、そのほかに when, why, how があります。

a) 関係副詞 when の例 :
I still remember the day <u>when</u> I first met my wife.
「私は今でも妻に最初に会った日のことを覚えている。」

関係副詞 when は、時を表す先行詞を説明する節を作ります。上の例では先行詞 the day について、「私が妻に最初に会った」日であることを説明しています。

b) 関係副詞 why の例 :
The reason (<u>why</u>) I'm a comedian is because I'm a fan of comedy.
「私がコメディアンである理由は、コメディーのファンであるからです。」

関係副詞 why の先行詞になり得るのは事実上 (the) reason「理由」だけであり、why で始まる節がその内容を説明しますが、why 自体はしばしば省略されます。

c) 関係副詞 how の例 :
This is <u>how</u> we solved the problem.

「このようにして我々はその問題を解決しました。」

関係副詞 how は「方法・様態」を表し、理論上は the way という先行詞があるものと考えられますが、実際には先行詞なしで用いられます。（ただし、how を使わずに the way を使って "This is the way we solved the problem." という文は可能です。）

4　Listen to the dialogue and fill in the blanks.

会話文の音声を聞き、空所に適切な語をいれなさい。

Daichi: Hi, Mika. I went to an international students' party last Sunday. I met some Indonesian girls studying engineering at college. They were all wearing headscarves.

Mika: Oh, you mean the hijab? Muslim women have to wear one in (1.　　　　).

Daichi: Oh, really? Why?

Mika: Strict Muslims believe women should not show certain parts of their body, such as the face, hair and neck, to men who are not their family members. They should be (2.　　　　) from other men, so it's like a rule for Muslim women to wear the hijab when they go outside. It demonstrates their modesty and belief in God. But did you know France banned the wearing of face veils in public schools in 2004?

Daichi: Do you mean elementary and secondary schools?

Mika: Yes, state schools up to the age of eighteen. The law prohibits not only (3.　　　　) face veils but any display of religious identity, whatever the religion, for example, crucifixes, which some Christians wear.

Daichi: What was the (4.　　　　) of people in France and other countries to this law?

Mika: Well, most support it, but some don't. They say people's religious beliefs and how they express them should be protected. People should have the freedom to practice their faith as long as they do so peacefully.

Daichi: I understand their point.

Mika: However, most French people support the law. They believe state schools should be free from religion and that all children should feel equal. When in school they should feel French first and foremost, rather than members of a religious group.

Daichi: I read France has about five million Muslims, the largest Muslim population in the Western world. I hear the French government encourages immigrants to be (5.   ) into French society.

Mika: You're right. As French citizens, they are expected to learn about the country's history, traditions, and culture so they can integrate more easily.

Daichi: What do you think of France's decision to ban the wearing of face veils in public schools?

5 What's your opinion?

Daichi の問いかけに、自分の考えを述べてみましょう。

Daichi: What do you think of France's decision to ban wearing face veils in public schools?

You: I think _____ because _____.

次の❻ Cultural Information: Do you know? も参考にしてください。

6 Cultural Information: Do you know?

ステレオタイプ（stereotype）

　ステレオタイプとは、人間の内面にある固定観念をさし、生得的なものではなく、社会化の過程で学んでいきます。私たちの心的内面には、情報をカテゴリー別に分類し、整理する認知的な働きがあります。これには良い面と悪い面があります。良い面としては、この情報過多の時代で、認知資源（覚えるデータ容量）が限られている場合、すべて詳細な情報を覚えようとするよりは、分類され整理した情報から取捨選択して外界を見る方が便利で、時間が節約できます。しかし、悪い面として、私たちは、この単純化され、極端化しがちの情報を、知らず知らずのうちに、自分の判断や行動の参考にしてしまうことがあげられます。

（八島智子・久保田真弓, 2012）

　人を分類するときの基準は、特に異文化コミュニケーションにおいては、

注意を要します。「アメリカ人は——」「イタリア人は——」と対象のグループを単純化し、一般的してしまい、全員が同じ特徴を持っているように考えてしまうことです。このステレオタイプに否定的な見方が加わると、望ましいコミュニケーションが阻止されます。目の前の人をしっかり把握するために、もう一度、自分の持っているステレオタイプを冷静に見直し、事実を正確に判断するように情報を求めていきましょう。

（八代京子・荒木昌子　他，2011）

✏ Related Vocabulary

inherent, innate: 生得的な　acquired: 後天的な　categorize: ～を分類する　simplify: 単純化する　prejudice: 偏見　a positive view: 肯定的な見方　a negative view : 否定的な見方　break (stereotypes): (ステレオタイプを) 打ち破る

CHAPTER 13

Finland Named The World's Happiest Country

毎年発表される世界幸福度ランキングで、日本は数年間順位を下げ続けています。どのような国が幸福だと評価されているのでしょうか。

Finland is the world's happiest country. The World Happiness Report, published Wednesday, studied the happiness levels of 156 countries. It considered factors such as life expectancy, social support, and corruption in its examination.

Finland pushed last year's happiest country, Norway, to second place. The other three Nordic countries — Denmark, Sweden, and Iceland — also made the top ten. They are joined by Switzerland, The Netherlands, Canada, New Zealand, and Australia.

For the first time, the report also ranked 117 countries by the happiness and well-being of their foreign-born immigrants. Finland placed first in that group as well. In fact, the study found that highly ranked countries in overall happiness had similarly happy immigrant populations.

John Helliwell is an editor of the 2018 World Happiness Report. He said the study shows that a population's happiness seems contagious. In other words, it spreads. He called that the "most striking finding" of the report. "Those who move to happier countries gain, while those who move to less happy countries lose," Helliwell said.

Finland is a nation of 5.5 million people. It has about 300,000 foreigners. Its largest immigrant groups come from other European countries. But there are also small communities from Afghanistan, China, Iraq, and Somalia.

Meik Wiking is chief of the Happiness Research Institute, based in Denmark's capital, Copenhagen. He said that Nordic countries almost always rank near the top of the happiness report. He said they are, in his words, "doing something right in terms of creating good conditions for good lives." He said the findings on the happiness of immigrants, "show the conditions that we live under matter greatly to our quality of life, that happiness is not only a matter of choice."

The United States ranked 11th in the first World Happiness report, released in 2012, but it has never been in the top 10. The U.S. fell to 18th place this year, after ranking 14th in 2017.

The report noted several reasons for its falling position. It said the United States is in the middle of "a complex and worsening public health crisis, involving...obesity, opioid addiction, and major depressive disorder." It added that the sociopolitical system in the U.S. produces more income inequality — a major reason for unhappiness — than other countries with similarly high income levels. (378 words)

📝 NOTE

The World Happiness Report: 世界幸福度報告　life expectancy: 平均寿命
well-being: 快適さ、満足感、充実感、健康等が良好的な状態であること、幸福
Nordic countries: 北欧　quality of life: 生活の質　opioid addiction: オピオイ
ド（鎮痛・陶酔作用がある化合物）依存症　depressive disorder: うつ病性障害
sociopolitical system : 社会政治的制度

How many words do you know?

次の単語の意味を、右の選択肢から選び記号で答えなさい。

1. factor	(	)	a. 広がる
2. corruption	(	)	b. 顕著な、著しい
3. striking	(	)	c. ～を公表する
4. contagious	(	)	d. 肥満
5. spread	(	)	e. 不正
6. release	(	)	f. 要因
7. obesity	(	)	g. (感情・態度・思想が) 人に移りやすい

Reading Comprehension: True or False

次の英文が、本文の内容に合っていればTを、合っていなければFを（　　）
内に書きなさい。

1. The World Happiness Report does not consider how long people are expected to live in each country. （　　）

2. The ranking of countries by the happiness of their immigrants differed greatly from the ranking of countries by overall happiness. （　　）

3. According to John Helliwell, immigrants who move to happier countries seem to be happier than those who move to less happy countries. （　　）

4. Meik Wiking thinks Nordic countries are not accepting enough immigrants. （　　）

5. According to the report, the gap between the rich and poor in the United States is one of the reasons for its relatively low rank. （　　）

3 Grammar section

「前置詞をともなう関係代名詞」
The conditions <u>that</u> we live <u>under</u> matter greatly to our quality of life.
「我々が生活する条件は、我々の生活の質にとってたいへん重要である。」

上の文では、関係代名詞 that で始まり、前置詞 under で終わる節 "that we live under"「その下で我々が生活する」が先行詞 "the conditions"「条件」を修飾し、「（その下で）我々が生活する条件」という意味になって文の主語になっています。（この文の動詞は matter「重要である」です。）

また、上の文の関係代名詞 that は which に置き換えることもできますが、その場合には前置詞が関係詞節の最後に置かれるパターンと、前置詞が関係代名詞の直前に置かれるパターンの二通りが可能です。

a) which + 前置詞後置の例：
　The conditions <u>which</u> we live <u>under</u> matter greatly to our quality of life.

b) 前置詞 + which の例：
　The conditions <u>under which</u> we live matter greatly to our quality of life.

なお、上の a の例では、関係代名詞 which を省略することが可能です。

a はどちらかと言えば会話などでよく使われるやや口語的表現（関係代名詞を省略するとさらに口語的）、b は文章でよく使われるやや堅い表現になります。（前置詞 + that という形は不可。）

ところで前置詞 + which という形は、多くの場合、関係副詞の when や where で置き換えることができます。b の文は関係副詞の where を使って書き換えることが可能で、次のようになります。

c) 関係副詞の where を使った例 :

The conditions <u>where</u> we live matter greatly to our quality of life.

4　Listen to the dialogue and fill in the blanks.

会話文の音声を聞き、空所に適切な語をいれなさい。

Yuka:　Hi, Daichi. I took a trip to Finland with my friend during winter vacation.

Daichi:　Oh, that's wonderful! I'm very interested in Nordic countries. The (1.　　　　　) of life is very high and (2.　　　　) is highly valued .

Yuka:　Yes, that's right. Finland is the happiest country in the world.

Daichi:　What city did you visit in Finland, Yuka?

Yuka:　Our final destination was Rovaniemi, the capital city of Lapland. Can you believe the city is just four miles south of the Arctic Circle? As far as I could see, everything was (3.　　　　) with snow. To my surprise, it was dark as night in the daytime.

Daichi:　That's the "polar night." The sun doesn't rise above the horizon during the winter months in the northernmost parts of Europe.

Yuka:　Right. It made me feel depressed, though. Anyway, after arriving in Rovaniemi we took a bus tour to explore Lapland.

Daichi:　That sounds interesting. Tell me more.

Yuka:　First, we went to Santa Claus Village. You know, it's open all the year round. We met Santa Claus and had a picture taken with him. After that, we enjoyed an adventure in the snow-covered world, riding in a reindeer sleigh and then on a snowmobile.

Daichi:　You really had some exciting experiences there, didn't you? Well,

Yuka, what was the most (4.   ) tour experience?

Yuka: Aurora borealis, the northern lights! We searched for the northern lights in the sky at night. It was very cold outside, though, so sometimes we went back to the house to warm ourselves by the fireplace. I can't fully describe the moment when we saw green lights start to (5.   ) all over the dark sky. The stars were still twinkling under a bright green veil. I'll never forget it!

Daichi: Amazing! It's truly a wonder of nature.

Yuka:　What would you like to do if you took a trip to Finland, Daichi?

5　**What's your opinion?**

Yuka の問いかけに、自分の考えを述べてみましょう。

Yuka: What would you like to do in Finland?

You: I would like to _____ .

次の❻ Cultural Information: Do you know? も参考にしてください。

6　**Cultural Information: Do you know?**

世界幸福度報告（The World Happiness Report）

　世界幸福度報告（The World Happiness Report）は、国際幸福デーの3月20日に、国連が毎年発表している幸福度のランキングレポートで、第一回目の報告は2012年4月に出版されました。この調査における幸福度とは、各国の人に、「どのくらい幸せと感じているのか」を0から10の段階で評価した世論調査に、GDP、平均余命、寛大さ、社会的支援、自由度、腐敗度などの要素を元に、幸福度をはかっています。

　2018年、2019年、2020年は3年続けてフィンランドが第一位でした。日本は、2010年代前半は40位台でしたが、後半には50位台に落ち、2019年58位、2020年は過去最低の62位でした。

World Happiness Report 2019

::

No. 1　　フィンランド　(Finland)

No. 2　　デンマーク (Denmark)

No. 3　　ノルウェー　(Norway)

No. 4　　アイスランド　(Iceland)

No. 5　　オランダ　(the Netherlands)

No. 6　　スイス　(Switzerland)

No. 7　　スェーデン　(Sweden)

No. 8　　ニュージーランド　(New Zealand)

No. 9　　カナダ　(Canada)

No. 10　　オーストリア　(Austria)

::

（世界幸福度ランキング 2019，Nobuyuki Kokai，2019）

✎ Related Vocabulary

make a survey of public opinion: 世論調査をする　social welfare system: 社会福祉制度　medical expenses: 医療費　tax rate: 税率　tuition fees: 授業料 free: 無料の　autonomy, independence: 自主性　scholastic (academic) ability gap: 学力格差

CHAPTER 14

New Zealand Celebrates Women's Suffrage Anniversary

当たり前に思われることが当たり前ではないことを思い出すのが「記念日」といえる
かもしれません。「当たり前」だと思う身の回りの物事についても考えてみましょう。
（写真は第40代ニュージーランド首相ジャシンダ・アーダーン）
New Zealand Government, Office of the Governor-General

New Zealand has marked the 125th anniversary of a historic move to give women the vote. In September 1893, New Zealand passed the Electoral Act, which gave women over the age of 21 the right to vote in parliamentary elections. It was the first country to do so, and this move represented a significant milestone on the path to gender equality.

In parliament, Prime Minister Jacinda Ardern, New Zealand's third female prime minister, promised the nation's 19th century fight for economic independence and equal rights for women would continue and praised the campaigners who had brought about fundamental change all those years ago.

"First and foremost, as a tribute to the women who led the change — to Kate Sheppard; to Margaret Seabright; to the 25,000 women who signed the petition in 1893—I move that this house mark the 125th anniversary of New Zealand women becoming the first in the world to win the right to vote, and celebrate the contribution of women to New Zealand's democracy, past, present, and future," said Ardern.

Schools, theaters, museums, and libraries have hosted events commemorating the world-first legislation and discussions about how to achieve greater equality. Issues that need to be addressed include the economic disparity between men and women and the preponderance of men at the senior management level.

The gender pay gap in the South Pacific nation is, on average, 10%. Working mothers are at an even greater disadvantage, having to contend with a salary difference of about 17% between them and their male peers — a pay difference known as the "motherhood penalty". Women are also under-represented in some senior corporate positions. Among New Zealand's top 50-listed companies, female executives make up just a fifth of directors and, although about 40% of New Zealand lawmakers are women, less than a third of government ministers are female.

A union representing public service workers in New Zealand has held an equal pay strike demanding an end to wage discrimination. The center-left Ardern government, which came to power a year ago, has also this week brought in new laws designed to make it easier for female employees to make claims for equal pay. (360 Words)

📝 NOTE

suffrage: 参政権　Electoral Act: 選挙法　1893 年、ニュージーランドの国会で女性の一般選挙参政権を認めた法律　parliamentary election: 議会選挙　gender equality: 男女平等　Jacinda Ardern: 第 40 代ニュージーランド首相　as a tribute to the women: 女性に敬意を表して　Kate Sheppard：ニュージーランドの女性参政権論者　preponderance: 優勢　senior corporate positions: (企業の) 上級幹部の地位

---

1 **How many words do you know?**

次の単語の意味を、右の選択肢から選び記号で答えなさい。

1. milestone	(　　)	a. (国会) 議員
2. praise	(　　)	b. 不利益
3. commemorate	(　　)	c. 画期的な事件
4. petition	(　　)	d. 格差
5. disparity	(　　)	e. 嘆願書
6. disadvantage	(　　)	f. 〜を称賛する
7. lawmaker	(　　)	g. 〜を祝う

2 Reading Comprehension: True or False

次の英文が、本文の内容に合っていればTを、合っていなければFを（　　）内に書きなさい。

1. No country in the world gave women the right to vote until 1893. (　　)

2. Jacinda Ardern praised only Kate Sheppard and Margaret Seabright for their contribution to win women's right to vote. (　　)

3. There are still some inequalities between men and women in New Zealand. (　　)

4. The "motherhood penalty" refers to the fact that working mothers tend to receive lower salaries than women without children. (　　)

5. Gender parity is closer to being achieved in business than in politics. (　　)

3 Grammar section

「二重目的語」（第4文型）
The Electoral Act gave <u>women over the age of 21</u> <u>the right to vote in parliamentary elections</u>.
「選挙法は、21歳を超える女性に議会選挙で投票する権利を与えた。」

上の文では、<u>women over the age of 21</u>「21歳を超える女性」が動詞 give の間接目的語、<u>the right to vote in parliamentary elections</u>「議会選挙で投票する権利」が直接目的語となっています。

間接目的語には多くの場合、人を表す表現が入り、「〜に」という意味を表すのに対し、直接目的語には多くの場合、物・事を表す表現が入り、「〜を」という意味を表します。

間接目的語と直接目的語の2つの目的語（二重目的語）を取る典型的な動詞としては、give のほか、lend「貸す」pay「支払う」sell「売る」teach「教える」tell「話す」などがあります。なお、二重目的語を持つ文型を通例「第4文型」と呼びます。

また、第4文型の文は、間接目的語と直接目的語の位置を入れ替え、間接目

的語の前に前置詞 to を置く形に書き換えることが可能で、上の文は次のよううに書き換えが可能です。

The Electoral Act gave <u>the right to vote in parliamentary elections</u> <u>to</u> <u>women over the age of 21</u>.

ただし、この場合には前置詞 to 以下の部分は前置詞句とみなされ、動詞 give の目的語ではなくなるので、文型としては目的語を一つだけ持つ「第3文型」となります。
ところで、二重目的語を取る動詞の中でも、buy「買う」make「作る」find「見つける」get「手に入れる」などの場合は、第4文型から第3文型への書き換えの際に、前置詞として to ではなく for を用います。
He bought <u>his girlfriend</u> <u>an expensive necklace</u>.（第4文型）
「彼は自分の彼女に高価なネックレスを買ってあげた。」
⇒ He bought <u>an expensive necklace</u> <u>for</u> <u>his girlfriend</u>.（第3文型）

4　Listen to the dialogue and fill in the blanks.

会話文の音声を聞き，　空所に適切な語をいれなさい。

Daichi: Hi, Mika. What are you looking at?

Mika:　Hi, Daichi. It's a map of New Zealand. Japan and New Zealand are in (1.　　　　　) hemispheres, so it's winter there when we're swimming in the sea!

Daichi: Yes, I learned that at school. So if you (2.　　　　) skiing, you should go there in our summer! Anyway, why are you looking at a map of New Zealand?

Mika:　I'd like to go someday. I'm very interested in women's issues there.

Daichi: Oh, yeah? Why?

Mika:　I saw on the news that New Zealand's prime minister, Jacinda Ardern, is visiting Japan. It seems she was just 37 years old when she became their third female prime minister.

Daichi: You mean three women have had the top job in the country? Awesome!

Mika:　And she became the first prime minister in the world to take maternity leave.

Daichi: Oh, really? I wonder whether her partner took paternity leave, too.

Mika:　I have no idea. Did you know that New Zealand was the first country to grant women's (3.   )? That was in 1893. It was a really long, hard, seven-year struggle led by a woman named Kate Sheppard.

Daichi: Respect! That was during the Meiji era in Japan, wasn't it? What's the percentage of female (4.   ) in parliament now?

Mika: About 40%. Their target number is 50%. That compares to about 15% in Japan. I think we should be more serious about promoting (5.   ) equality policies.

Daichi: You said it! Is there a government department responsible for supporting women's rights in New Zealand?

Mika: Yes. Appropriately, it's called the Ministry for Women. It was founded in 1984 to bring women's voices to government and give advice to policymakers about issues relating to women.

Daichi: Great! After talking with you, Mika, I've become more curious about New Zealand. Do you know anything else about the country?

5 What's your opinion?

Daichi の問いかけに、自分の考えを述べてみましょう。

Daichi: Do you know anything more about New Zealand?

You: _____ .

次の❻ Cultural Information: Do you know? も参考にしてください。

6 Cultural Information: Do you know?

ニュージーランドの女性参政権

　21世紀前期の現在、世界の大部分の国々で国政レベルの女性参政権が確立し、女性の参政権が当たりまえだと思われています。ニュージーランドでは1893年の国政レベルの選挙で、世界で最初に参政権（投票権）が実現しました。ケイト・シェパード（Katherine W. Sheppard）という一人の女性参政権論者のリードにより押し進められた選挙改正法案は、何度も否決され、成立するまでの7年間にわたる過程は平凡でなく、長く困難な道でした。1893年に、成人女性の4分の1にあたる3万人以上の嘆願書の署名が議会に提出され、女性に選挙権を付与するための選挙改正法案が国会を通過したとき、

世界中の女性活動家が歓喜したと言われています。

　ニュージーランドは多文化国家のため、ニュージーランド女性といっても、ヨーロッパ系からマリオ系、太平洋諸島民系、アジア系などの違いもあれば、障害を持つ女性、移民の女性など様々な多様性があることが認識されており、全員に公平な機会を与えるためにそれぞれに応じたアプローチ法が求められています。ニュージーランドは、男女共同参画の分野で、世界を牽引してきました。ジェンダー・ギャップ指数も高評価を得るまでの変遷をたどってきました。

　ニュージーランドの教員アリソン・クーパーとジュディ・パティンソンは、「開拓時代に女性が男性と一緒に汗を流して働いた実績が、女性のための制度の確立の背景になっている」と述べています。女性の被選挙権獲得は、それから26年後の1919年に認められ、1947年に初の女性閣僚が誕生し、保険大臣と児童福祉大臣を務めました。

　2017年10月に37歳の若さで、ジャシンダ・アーダーン（Jacinda Ardern）がニュージーランドで3人目の女性首相として就任し、女性閣僚の占める比率が高い内閣が発足しました。

（CLAIR 一般財団法人自治体国際化協会，2015年）

📝 Related Vocabulary

a land of immigrants: 移民の国　constitutional monarchy: 立憲君主制　the South Pacific: 南太平洋　governor-general: 総督　population density: 人口密度　the Southern Cross: 南十字星　endangered species: 絶滅危惧種 ecosystem: 生態系

CHAPTER 15

Political Cartoons: Exploring Serious Subjects in a Fun Way

漫画は楽しむためだけのものではなく、メッセージを伝える１つの手段でもあります。SNS の世界でも風刺漫画を見かけることが多いです。作者はどのような思いで制作しているのでしょうか。

Political cartoons date back to before the founding of the United States and remain an important part of American culture. Under the First Amendment to the U.S. Constitution they are protected as part of a free press.

Matt Wuerker is a long-time political cartoonist, whose work appears in Politico, a media company that reports on U.S. politics. A 2012 Pulitzer Prize winner, he sees his job as quite unusual. "We're a strange mix of things, in that we are making serious commentary on serious topics, but we're doing it not so seriously."

Wuerker likes the fact that he can express opinions in the same way as television commentators and those who write opinion pieces for newspapers. The difference, he says, is that he gets to create what he calls "silly pictures" to get his point across.

Wuerker has seen many changes in the publishing industry over the years. When he started 40 years ago, political cartoons appeared as simple, black and white images in newspapers. Today, they are more colorful, or even animated. Some cartoonists have created whole illustrated stories about political subjects. One such, called "Welcome to the New World," is currently being shown at the Newseum in Washington. It tells of two refugee families from Syria who came to the United States. Created by Michael Sloan and Jake Halpern, it won a 2018 Pulitzer Prize.

Officials at the Newseum liked what they saw, according to Patty Rhule, vice president of exhibits there. "They did a 20-part series in The New York Times following the story of two Syrian immigrants who fled the war in Syria to come to this country and start a new life with their families."

Rhule said news-related cartoons have always been an important part of

American culture. The country's first political cartoon is generally considered to be one by Benjamin Franklin, a founding father, and showed a snake cut into parts. Published in 1754, it was meant to increase support for his plan for a union of Britain's North American colonies.

Rhule says she hopes this long tradition will live on for many years to come. "It's always been a part of this country and the world's way of freely expressing ideas and debate. So I hope they never go away." (374 words)

✎ NOTE

political cartoons: 風刺漫画　the First Amendment to the U.S. Constitution: アメリカ合衆国憲法修正第一条　Matt Wuerker: マット・ワーカー　アメリカの政治漫画家　Politico: ポリティコ　アメリカの政治に特化したニュースメディア　Newseum: ニュージアム　アメリカの首都ワシントン D.C. にあったニュースとジャーナリズムに関する博物館　２０１９年に閉館　"Welcome to the New World"（新世界へようこそ）：アメリカのイラストレーター　Michael Sloan（マイケル・スローン）とアメリカの著作家 Jake Halpern（ジェイク・ハルパーン）の作品で、2018 年、ピューリッツァー賞時事漫画部門を受賞　Benjamin Franklin: アメリカ合衆国の建国の父の1人

1　**How many words do you know?**

次の単語の意味を、右の選択肢から選び記号で答えなさい。

1. serious	(　　)	a. 漫画家
2. commentary	(　　)	b. 難民
3. silly	(　　)	c. 解説
4. animated	(　　)	d. 展示会
5. cartoonist	(　　)	e. 真面目な
6. refugee	(　　)	f. ばかげた
7. exhibit	(　　)	g. アニメーションの

2　Reading Comprehension: True or False

次の英文が、本文の内容に合っていれば T を、合っていなければ F を（　　）内に書きなさい。

1. Political cartoons existed prior to the foundation of the United States.
（　　）

2. According to Matt Wuerker, he does his job in exactly the same way as television commentators.
（　　）

3. Political cartoons have changed a lot over the last 40 years.
（　　）

4. Patty Rhule is the cartoonist who created the illustrated story about two refugee families from Syria.
（　　）

5. Benjamin Franklin used the image of a snake cut into pieces to get his political message across.
（　　）

3　Grammar section

「同格表現」

The country's first political cartoon is generally considered to be one by Benjamin Franklin, a founding father.

「米国で最初の政治漫画は一般に、建国の父の一人であるベンジャミン・フランクリンによるものと考えられている。」

上の文では、固有名詞 Benjamin Franklin の後に、カンマで区切ってその人物についての補足説明として a founding father「（米国の）建国の父」という名詞句を続けています。このように、ある名詞（句）の後にカンマ（,）、ダッシュ（–）、セミコロン（;）、コロン（:）などで区切って補足説明や言い換えとなる名詞（句）を続けることを「同格表現」と呼びます。

「同格表現」という呼び名は、最初の名詞（句）と、それに続く名詞（句）が、文法的に同じ格になっていることから来ています。（上の例文では、ともに前置詞 by の後で目的格になっています。）
同格表現の関係は、名詞（句）と名詞（句）との間に成り立つだけでなく、名詞（句）と名詞節（ほとんどの場合は that 節）との間にも成り立ちます。（この場合には間にカンマなどは入りません。）

Wuerker likes the fact that he can express opinions in the same way as television commentators.

「ワーカー氏は、自分がテレビコメンテーターと同じやり方で意見を表明することができるという事実を気に入っている。」

この例では、the fact「事実」という名詞句について、その詳しい内容を後ろの同格の that 節が説明して「・・・という事実」という意味になっています。

後ろに同格の that 節を従えることができる典型的な名詞には、fact のほかに news「ニュース」、idea「考え」、announcement「発表」、claim「主張」、demand「要求」などがあります。

4 Listen to the dialogue and fill in the blanks.

会話文の音声を聞き、空所に適切な語をいれなさい。

Linda: Hi, Daichi. Look at this book. It's a 2018 Pulitzer Prize-winning comic book.

Daichi: Let's see…"Welcome to the New World." Oh, it looks interesting. Who created it?

Linda: The writer was Jake Halpern and the cartoonist Michael Sloan. It's a nonfiction work about a Syrian (1.   ) family who seek freedom in the U.S. Jake Halpern met the family a number of times to do research for the book.

Daichi: Oh, it's a true story? It sounds interesting.

Linda: It is…you should read it. It's what's called a political cartoon, a form of (2.   ) on society and politics that allows people to criticize power and authority in a (3.   ) way. These cartoons play a very important role in American culture and are a sign of a healthy (4.   ).

Daichi: Oh, I see. What issues interest political cartoonists in the U.S.?

Linda: Wars, gender equality, Black people's rights, and environmental issues, to name a few. By the way, are there any political cartoons in Japan?

Daichi: Yes, there are. There are books of them, and you can find them in (5.   ) and magazines as well. They express ordinary people's fears, complaints and frustrations, just as they do in the U.S. In the past, they were anonymous, but not now. You know, I feel less frustrated and stressed whenever I see funny portraits and illustrations, and ironic captions.

Linda: Can you give me some names of famous political cartoonists?

Daichi: Well, Yukiyoshi Tokoro, Masaaki Sato and Shouji Yamafuji are very well known.

Linda: I'd like to take a look at their work.

Daichi: I'm curious to hear what you think. I'm interested in cartoons about gender equality. How about you, Linda? What topics are you interested in?

5 What's your opinion?

Daichi の問いかけに、自分の考えを述べてみましょう。

Daichi: What social and political topics are you interested in?

You: I am interested in _____ because _____ .

次の ❻ Cultural Information: Do you know? も参考にしてください。

6 Cultural Information: Do you know?

アメリカの風刺漫画

　独立戦争に備え、創立の父、ベンジャミン・フランクリンが民衆の結束を呼び掛ける画が描かれて以来、アメリカの風刺漫画は、アメリカの歴史と切り離せない文化となりました。常に体制に抵抗し、政治の腐敗や権力乱用を鋭く批判し、社会の意識向上に貢献する民主主義の自浄作用を助ける重要な手段です。アメリカでは表現や報道の自由は民主主義を支える上で重要な権利であるという認識がありますが、報道の自由を守るアメリカのメディアでも、なかには出版すべきかどうか判断のわかれる風刺画もあります。

（パトリック・ハーラン，2019 年）

comic strip: （新聞などに連載される）続き漫画　single frame comic : 一コマ漫画
four-frame comics: 四コマ漫画　political corruption: 政治の腐敗　power abuse:
権力の乱用　satire: 風刺　freedom of press: 報道の自由　freedom of speech:
表現の自由

マット・ワーカー氏の風刺漫画
作品の一つ

出典・参考文献一覧

Chapter 1

(1) 八島智子・久保田真弓 (2012).『異文化コミュニケーション論——グローバル・マインドとローカル・アフェクト』(pp. 4–7) 東京：松柏社.

(2) コミサロフ喜美 (2011)「3 異文化理解への態度」八代京子・荒木昌子・樋口容視子・山本志都・コミサロフ喜美 (2011).『異文化コミュニケーションワークブック』(pp. 17–19) 東京：三修社.

Chapter 2

(1) 金成玟 (2018).『K-POP 新感覚のメディア』(pp. 2–42) 東京：岩波書店.

(2) 酒井美絵子 (著) 鄭城尤 (監修) (2012).『なぜ K-POP スターは次から次に来るのか 韓国の恐るべき輸出戦略』東京：朝日新聞出版.

Chapter 3

(1) 国際 NGO プラン・インターナショナル「国際 ガールズ・デー 10 月 11 日」https://www.plan-international.jp/girl/girlsday (2020 年 1 月 15 日閲覧)

(2) UNICEF (2018) A Future stolen: Young and out-of-school〔盗まれた将来：学校に通っていないこどもたち〕https://data.unicef.org/resources/a-future-stolen/ (2020 年 1 月 25 日閲覧)

(3) 関橋眞理 (著) 公益財団法人プラン・ジャパン (監修) (2013).『世界の女性問題①貧困、教育、保健』(p. 24) 東京：汐文社.

Chapter 4

(1) 株式会社ヴァイキング (2009).『北大西洋諸国ガイドブック』東京：アイスランド航空日本総代理店・(株)ヴァイキング.

(2) 外務省 (2018).「アイスランド共和国 (Republic of Iceland) 基礎データ」https://www.mofa.go.jp/mofaj/area/iceland/data.html#section5 (2020 年 10 月 4 日閲覧)

Chapter 6

(1) ロー , リュシー (著) 別宮貞徳 (監訳) (2000).『世界の民族楽器文化図鑑』東京：柊風舎.

Chapter 7

(1) 鎌田 遵 (2009).『ネイティブ・アメリカン——先住民社会の現在』(pp. 129–134) 東京：岩波新書.

Chapter 8

(1) 碇 知子 (2017).「食料自給の向上に目を向け始めたシンガポール」公益財団法人ひろしま産業振興機構 https://www.hiwave.or.jp/wp-content/uploads/2017/08/rp-sg1708.pdf (2020 年 4 月 2 日閲覧)

Chapter 9

(1) 石川和博 (著) 松田素二・津田みわ (編者) (2012).『ケニアを知るための 55 章』(pp. 171–174) 東京：明石書店.

(2) 斎藤道雄 (2016).『手話を生きる——少数言語が多数派日本語と出会うところで』東京：みすず書房.

Chapter 10

（1）名古屋検疫所 https://www.forth.go.jp/keneki/nagoya/（2020 年 5 月 2 日閲覧）

（2）東山安子（2020）『英語教師のためのコミュニケーション読本　Verbal & Nonverbal Communication』（pp. 22–23, p. 171, p. 195）Parade Books.

Chapter 11

（1）マーティン, ダニエラ（著）梶山あゆみ（訳）（2016）.『私が虫を食べるわけ』東京：飛鳥新社.

（2）テーブズ, デイビッド・ウォルトナー（著）片岡夏実（訳）（2019）.『昆虫食と文明：昆虫の新たな役割を考える』東京：築地書館.

Chapter 12

（1）八島智子・久保田真弓（2012）.『異文化コミュニケーション論――グローバル・マインドとローカル・アフェクト』（pp. 239–240）東京：松柏社.

（2）八代京子（2011）「2　ステレオタイプ」八代京子・荒木昌子・樋口容視子・山本志都・コミサロフ喜美『異文化コミュニケーションワークブック』（pp. 15–16）東京：三修社.

Chapter 13

（1）Kokai, Nobuyuki（2019）.　世界幸福度ランキング 2019（World Happiness Report 2019）日本 58位　https://kokai.jp/ 世界幸福度ランキング 2019（world-happiness-report-2019）日本 58 位 /（2020年 6 月 10 日閲覧）

（2）Helliwell, John F., Layard, Richard, & Sachs, Jeffry D.（2019）.　World Happiness Report 2019, New York: Sustainable Development Solutions Network. https://worldhappiness.report/ed/2019/（2020 年 6 月 10 日閲覧）

Chapter 14

（1）（一財）自治体国際化協会シドニー事務所（2015）.「CLAIR REPORT No. 410　ニュージーランドにおける女性の社会参画」（pp. 7–8）http://www.clair.or.jp/j/forum/pub/docs/410.pdf（2020 年 6 月25 日閲覧）

（2）Ministry for Women (n.d.). https://women.govt.nz/（2020 年 6 月 29 日閲覧）

Chapter 15

（1）ハーラン, パトリック（2019 年 7 月 9 日）.「残念過ぎる風刺漫画の掲載中止」Newsweek 日本語版（p. 49）

テキストの音声は、弊社 HP
http://www.eihosha.co.jp/
の「テキスト音声ダウンロード」の
バナーからダウンロードできます。

VOA News: Readings for Cross-cultural Understanding
異文化理解のための VOA ニュース 15

2021 年 1 月 15 日　初　版
2023 年 2 月 28 日　2　刷

瀧 由紀子　中島 和郎
編　著　者　Jay Ercanbrack　Jonathan Jackson
榎本 暁　齊藤 隆春　山内 優佳

発　行　者　佐々木　元

発　行　所　株式会社　英　　宝　　社
〒101-0032 東京都千代田区岩本町 2-7-7
TEL 03 (5833) 5870-1 FAX 03 (5833) 5872

ISBN 978-4-269-19040-5 C1082

[製版：伊谷企画／印刷・製本：モリモト印刷株式会社]